FIX YOUR GARDEN

HOW TO MAKE SMALL SPACES INTO GREEN OASES

JANE MOSELEY & JACKIE STRACHAN

ILLUSTRATIONS BY CLAIRE ROLLET

PORTICO

CONTENTS

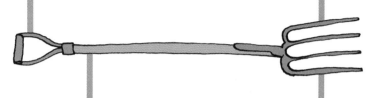

INTRODUCTION

Congratulations. You've moved into your new home. You can see the wood from the trees indoors and now you're looking out of the window at your outdoor patch and thinking about how to bring green and pleasant things to it. It may be a small plot or a collection of tubs and pots, but fret not. Green oases can be found in very small spaces, and indeed, you don't even have to have a garden to garden; the no-garden garden is a blossoming concept. A simple tree in a tub makes a green, architectural and environmental statement. Your area doesn't have to tick all the boxes, but one or two of these will apply and help shape rather than lose the plot (and we deal with them all in this book):

- ☑ Patio
- ☑ Balcony
- ☑ Lawn
- ☑ Roof terrace
- ☑ Steps
- ☑ Pots and tubs
- ☑ Deck
- ☑ Walls
- ☑ Front garden
- ☑ Wilderness
- ☑ Land as far as the eye can see...

CHAPTER ONE
USING THE PLOT

Slug

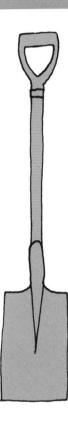

GREEN SPACES IN DIFFERENT PLACES

First things first, are you in the city or the country? A quick look out of the window should confirm. Urban gardens tend to be smaller and often shadier than their rural counterparts simply because of the available space and higher housing density (gardens can be higher too, on balconies, steps and rooftops, and lower, in basements and side passages). You might want to make your urban space, whatever its dimensions or shape, incline or outline, an extension of the interior, an enjoyable, peaceful, functional roofless room.

Ps AND Qs

Purpose, privacy and people (nosy/nice neighbours); peace and pollution (noise and environmental); planting potential; and lastly, but very importantly, pocket. Ask yourself lots of questions. How much do you have to spend? What is your proposed design? Does it involve hard landscaping? Will you need professional help?

PRIVACY

This is likely to be an issue with other homes to the left, right, below or above, so you probably need to consider screening and noise reduction features. Think laterally. The more compact it is, the more open to all-round view and scrutiny, so make the most of every single metre of space. You will need to consider your near but not yet dear neighbours and the amount of shade you get from their space, from tall buildings, trees and street furniture. Creating a green screen delivers both colour and privacy (see page 106) to your plot and is a design feature in itself. Light will be a key factor for some plots so think about ways of unblocking it: an open, slatted fence will let in light and filter wind while keeping out prying eyes. An arch or pergola will help gardens that are overlooked.

SIZE

There are ways you can maximize the size of your garden: by clearing inherited features, painting walls to make best use of reflected sunshine (beware the bare glare of pure white), introducing sealed mirrors to give the illusion of space (one or a whole wall of them). A door in one corner can create the impression of a space beyond, Narnia-like. Think of all the surfaces, horizontal or vertical as potential gardening areas. Don't be a waster of space but don't eat it up with

stuff just because you brought it with you or are mirroring your living room. Less is often more and a few large, eye-catching plants in a very small garden tend to be better than lots of small ones.

STYLE

For a designer look, paint the walls a statement colour, even creating a *trompe l'oeil*, add stylish topiary and wall-mounted pots. Many urban gardens are long and narrow so use hedges and climbers rather than space-and-time-taking beds.

Minimalist Japanese-style gardens would work well in a hectic city environment; a space for quiet contemplation after a busy day. Go for harmony and balance in the various features. Make them work together and separately. Decking can make a kitchen out of an outdoor space. A big statement plant in each corner of the patio gives it structure and you can add low seating in the centre. Strategic use of solar-powered lights or lanterns helps with atmosphere. Go vertical (see page 104).

Country gardens can be front, back or side (like haircuts). Back gardens can lead into the countryside. A front garden brings privacy and protection from the road but it is also your welcome mat and showcase, so make the most of it with interesting paving, colourful pots and tubs, a bay tree or rose, trailing plants, hanging baskets or painted trellis for climbing plants. Opt for low-maintenance features to keep the garden smart if you are time-poor.

Coastal gardens will be subject to stronger winds with a dash of salt, greater sun exposure, different soil conditions (see page 16) and milder climes (in southern regions). A windbreak made of trees and shrubs is a good idea to provide shelter for seaside gardens, though bear in mind the shade it creates.

PATCH WORK

Get to know your plot. Measure it carefully, draw a sketch to scale (use the estate agent's details) and scan your drawings of the existing plot and your dream transformation into your tablet or pin your sketch to the refrigerator. Use one of the many garden apps or CAD programs that help you design on screen.

The size and shape of your garden will determine what you do in it, of course, but get to know which parts are in full sun or shady when, and how much moisture/wind you will get. Look at it from every angle and window (that may not take long) and consider its boundaries. Use your compass to establish which way it faces, look at how tall buildings and neighbouring trees affect the light during the day; how exposed is it? Take photographs at different times of the day or, if you can wait that long, in different seasons. If time and patience permit, don't tackle the garden immediately or you may regret a costly makeover. Leave it for a few weeks to watch how the sun moves around the garden and your ideas take root. Be nosy. Ask your neighbours for advice on what grows well for them, check out nearby gardens. Consider how the wind will affect your garden. Will you get sudden gusts or wind tunnels?

Think about whether you want flowers and/or vegetables. Are you planning to create a particular style (see Chapter 2) How much time will you have to look after it? Is encouraging wildlife a factor? Will you sit/dine/relax/play in it? Your second sketch may well change as you consider these factors.

If you are eager to get your trowel and spade out, work on a section at a time, starting in the most visible area. You can always make a moveable feast, a portable garden with containers of herbs and veg with pots and tubs on casters that you can move around later or according to the sun, wind and season. Nothing is fixed in concrete and you may save time and money in the long run.

RENTING OR OWNING?

First, check what your agreement allows you to do with your outdoor space and always consider safety issues (windowsills, balconies etc.). If you are renting, you may wonder about the benefits of investing time and money in creating a garden that is not yours, but you can take pots to your next home and a touch of green altruism is good for the environment and wildlife and does no harm to your karma. Always remember the neighbours.

NURSERY STEPS

Rushing off to the nursery to spend money on plants sounds like a good idea but hold your trolleys and horses. There are a number of ways of procuring plants (and those you actually need). Buy online or from mail order catalogues, both money-saving options. Consult experts at specialist and independent outlets for some good, face-to-face advice and check their useful websites.

TOP TIPS

Research Check which plants suit your conditions – in person at nurseries or on useful websites.

Check and select Choose good-quality, healthy-looking, well-shaped plants. Check for diseases and pests (see page 20). Always check the label for suitability.

Root of all evil Check that the main roots (whitish or tan) look fleshy and healthy with a good network of smaller fibrous roots (if present). Check the plants are not pot-bound, with roots so dense and matted that they fill the whole pot.

Think small Buy smaller plants – they are cheaper and will grow into bigger ones.

The market can be super Buy supermarket herbs and divide or share in return for, say, a different herb cutting. Check out offers at cut-price stores – there are some good bargains to be had.

Borrow Ask friends or neighbours for cuttings, extra plants they don't need, or suggest you share a larger order.

Local and vocal Visit local markets for some face-to-face growing tips and well-priced plants. Go to garden shows.

Corner the market Check out the bargain plants at garden centres and supermarkets and see if you can find some distressed, water-starved or pot-bound plants to nurture. They will need some TLC and know-how but will reward your pocket and green fingers.

Seeds of content The cheapest way to grow veg is from seed (see page 40). Buy these online, swap at local seed events or attend local fairs and garden shows. You can also save seeds from tomatoes and pumpkins, for example. Alternatively, buy young plants at a garden centre or nursery.

Plant it up You can buy ready-planted containers from supermarkets or nurseries but it is cheaper to choose and plant your own (see page 60).

Root of no evil Shallots, onions, leeks and other veg complete with roots purchased for consumption can be planted in compost.

Root and boot Garage and car-boot sales are useful sources of well-priced plants as are local community websites and listings.

Propagator motivator See page 38.

Layering, not forking out This works with climbers such as honeysuckle and clematis (see page 107). Check plants for trailing stems in the ground that have taken root in the soil and make a mini-plant. Dig this up, separate it from the main plant and replant (see page 47). It's a good wheeze with strawberries. Also for those that set seed and grow on their own, such as foxglove and columbine.

Divide and conquer Invest in large potful of perennials and divide (see page 60).

BASIC TOOLKIT

Try not to fork out lots of money on unnecessary tools. Buy only what you really need, depending on the size and nature of your garden and growing wish list (in both senses), and invest as much as you can in your selected items.

Choose with care and make sure your tools are durable and the right weight and height for you – thereby avoiding back strain – and for your hand size. Keep them sharp and rust-free by cleaning with steel wool or a wire brush. Wipe with an oily rag (boiled linseed oil works well) when you put them away and they will last for generations.

Spade For digging beds and holes, and for spreading manure or mulch ('T' handles are better for those with larger hands than 'D' handles; stainless steel, rust-resistant heads are also good). Not needed if you go the 'no dig' route (see page 62).
Fork For weeding and breaking up soil and lifting plants.
Dibber/trowel For planting seeds and moving seedlings.
Secateurs/pruning shears For pruning, taking cuttings for propagation and cutting wood that is not too thick. Bypass secateurs (two blades with a scissor-like action) are the most useful and are good for getting into small gaps, but the anvil type (one sharp blade that cuts down on a block) are good for hard, woody stems.

Watering can For all-important H_2O-ing, with a rose attachment for seedlings.
Gloves For protection.
Hoe For weed control. A Dutch hoe can slice the top of the weed and a draw hoe can pull weeds out of the ground.

Possible additions to your tool collection, depending on size and intention, are:

Garden rake For soil preparation, preparing seedbeds and removing debris. Good for lawns and leaf clearing, too.
Kneeling mat To make weeding as comfortable as possible.
Shears For clipping herbs and hedges.
Gardening knife For general cutting purposes, pruning and taking cuttings.
Garden scissors Don't use your kitchen ones.
Plastic trug For moving and collecting.
Wheelbarrow For moving and collecting on a grander scale.
Lawnmower If required (or borrow, share, hire).
Fertilizer
Garden twine
Multi-purpose, peat-free compost

Long-handled hoe

Spade

Bypass secateurs

Trowel

Gloves

Garden fork

Spade

Wellies

Watering can

SOILMATES

Get to know your soil type, its characteristics and its pH, which means its acidity or alkalinity, in order to determine which plants will fare best in your garden's conditions.

First, check how deep your soil is in various areas of the plot (it will be shallower near the perimeter) and add these measurements to your garden sketch. Does it feel very wet, or well-drained? Soils contain different levels of sand, silt and clay and are affected by the environment, rainfall and local temperatures. Most types can be improved with organic matter (see page 18) so keep your feet on the ground and don't despair, and remember you can create ideal conditions for your chosen plants and veg in contained plots, containers and raised beds. You can check plant labels to check suitability for your type of soil.

SOIL SURVIVOR
Rub the soil between your fingers to see how it feels.

Clay
If it's sticky and you can roll a small ball of moist soil into a sausage and make its ends meet in a ring, you are the proud owner of clay. Heavy and slow-draining, it gets waterlogged in winter and bakes hard in summer, but is usually very fertile. Suitable for growing roses, hydrangeas, day lilies (see rhs.org.uk for more).

Sandy
Sandy soil feels fine, dry and light, making digging easier. It is free-draining, so more demanding in terms of watering, and nutrients are washed away rather quickly; it tends to be acidic. Suitable for growing lavender, rosemary, thyme and Mediterranean plants.

pH ID

Each plot will have its own minerals, organic and inorganic matter and what you can grow will depend on this. The good news is that you can create your own ideal conditions in raised beds or containers. It is important to test the acidity or alkalinity of your soil before you do any new planting in the garden. Buy a simple pH test kit from the garden centre – they are not too pricey – and carry out the test in a couple of places if you have a largeish plot (in exposed and covered areas). You will probably find that your soil scores somewhere in the middle of a range that goes from pH1 (very acidic) to pH14 (highly alkaline). Acid soils have a pH of below seven, neutral is pH7 and alkaline is above seven. Your result will vary according to your location: inland, coastal, hot and cold climates.

Ericaceous plants need soil that is acid (with a low pH). They include camellia, rhododendron, azalea, heather, blueberry. If your soil is too alkaline, dig in a good quantity of ericaceous compost, or grow them in containers.

Silty

Silty soil feels fairly smooth. It is quite moisture-retentive and naturally fertile, though it compacts easily. It provides good growing conditions for most plants.

Loam

Loam is brown and crumbly and is usually viewed as the most desirable soil type. A mixture of clay, sand and silt, it manages to forge a path between the extremes of each type, like a soil ambassador.

Chalky

Chalky soil is very alkaline, affecting your choice of plants. It is normally very free-draining so dries out easily.

Peaty soil

Peaty soil is very dark. It can be wet in winter and is acidic, but supports growth well if lime is added.

BEDDING UP AND DOWN

You inherit your soil in a garden (a bit like your genes) but you can change things (unlike your genes), and the more you can do to keep it healthy, the more productive and attractive it will look. Work at it and you will reap the rewards.

DIGGING FOR VICTORY

Soil matters improve with matter. Well-rotted organic material, such as garden, farmyard or mushroom compost, improves drainage and adds nutrients. You can buy or make your own compost (see opposite) or try to find recycled green waste locally. Dig a layer of it into the soil with your fork.

Mulching is an effective way of improving soil. A top layer of about 5cm (2in) of garden compost, manure, bark chippings, seaweed or straw (for strawberries) keeps weeds from growing (mostly), helps the soil retain moisture in summer, deters pests and encourages beneficial organisms. Result. Apply it in spring and autumn. (Also, see page 65.)

A compost heap or bin is a gift that keeps on giving. Even if you have a very small space, you could have a wormery. A lightweight, simple and durable UV-treated plastic compost bin is probably the most practical option for limited budgets and spaces. More stylish alternatives include wooden or beehive designs. The humus you are making

COMPOST DOS AND DONTS

Spring into action Start composting in the spring for the best results, and mix nitrogen-rich soft green material (grass clippings, prunings, fresh leaves, etc.) with dry, brown, carbon-rich stuff (bark, dead leaves, scrunched-up newspaper).

Waste not, waste not Avoid including cooked food waste as it encourages vermin; vegetable and fruit trimmings are fine.

Don't make a meal of it Don't put in meat, bones, fish or dairy products for the reason above. Rinsed egg shells are fine, as are tea bags and coffee grounds.

Wooden it be nice Put some woody material at the bottom to help with air circulation.

Dump the lumps Don't chuck in great big chunks of cardboard or branches – shred them first or the compost will get indigestion.

Liquidate to aerate Spray with water to keep moist in the summer; this helps with the whole rotting business, but don't put too much wet and soggy stuff in, or it will be more like a soup kitchen.

Keep a lid on it This increases the heat and composting speed. Give it a turn with a fork from time to time, too.

Weed 'em out Don't put diseased plants or flowering or perennial weeds in, or you risk tiny bits of root or seeds re-growing again when you spread your homemade compost.

helps soil retain its moisture, adding nutrients and helping your garden and lawn grow. Plus you are recycling waste, creating an alternative to chemical fertilizers, and you don't have to worry about what to do with your lawn clippings.

OUT, DAMNED SPOT – BUGS AND DISEASES

The Slugs and Snails, the Earwigs and Aphids: they sound like a couple of new bands busking in your garden, and indeed they are not all that bad or unwelcome. Get to know the ones that you may want to go.

BLOT BLIGHTERS AND BUGS – OFFENDERS AND THE COUNTER-OFFENSIVES

We won't list them all or your green fingers may blanch, but there are a few pests you need to ID so you can say adieu. If you can spot the most common offenders and make regular inspections, you have more chance of nipping the problem in the bud. See the bug shots shown here for some of their ugly mugs.

MISS SLUG

Slugs and snails

ID Known collectively as garden molluscs.
Offence Make holes in everything they find, mostly at night and after rain. They like hostas, dahlias, sweet peas and tulips and top of their must-chew menu

of green side dishes are lettuce, celery, peas and beans.

Defence Do good things in the compost heap.

Remedy Encourage birds with their favourite plants and bird feeders (see page 84) and they will eat the slugs. Slug pellets *in extremis* – make sure they are not harmful to other wildlife (those with ferrous phosphates are approved by organic gardeners). Distract them with fruit skins or mugs of beer, or go out at night and find them (returning them to a safe new habitat if you can). Copper bands on containers of slug delicacies such as hostas can be effective.

Black spot

ID A fungal disease that causes dark spots and blotches on rose leaves and surfaces. Leaves turn yellow and drop off. Not fatal but the plant is weakened.

Offence Attacks roses, especially in warm, wet weather when spores spread, but doesn't kill them.

Defence None.

Remedy Remove affected leaves asap and throw away, but not into the compost.

Buy chemical spray that doesn't damage other wildlife.

Choose resistant varieties and prune out foliage at the end of the season. Not all roses get black spot, so check catalogues. Keep plants well fed.

Blight (late blight, potato/ tomato blight)

ID A nasty little fungal disease that forms brown patches on foliage, fruit or tubers of tomatoes and potatoes.

Offence Decimates toms and tatties, particularly during warm and humid weather. Leaves collapse and turn brown.

Defence None.

Remedy Remove the affected tomato leaves but you may find the leaf and stem both rot eventually, in which case dig up plants and throw them away (don't put in compost bin). Ditto with your tatties – once blight is in town (or country) it's green thumbs down for the blighted.

Plant seed potatoes from a reputable supplier and choose blight-resistant varieties. Maximize airflow around tomato plants and avoid getting water on the leaves.

Aphids (greenfly and blackfly)

ID Yellow, green, black, pink, white, mottled bugs. There are hundreds of different species of these little blighters.
Offence Suck sap, stunt growth and weaken plants, lurking under young leaves and on shoot tips, but they don't kill. Secrete honeydew which then attracts mould; leaves become blistered or contorted.
Defence Provide food for predators so part of ecosystem.
Remedy Just squash them by hand or hose off. Use insecticides in growing season if you must (such as insecticidal soft soap solution). Aphids on trees are practically untree-table.

Cabbage white larvae

ID Yellow and black, pale green or yellow-ish green caterpillars of the cabbage white butterfly.

Offence Make large holes in brassica crops (cabbages, cauliflowers, sprouts, swedes and turnips) and nasturtiums and leave brown deposits.
Defence Part of ecosystem.
Remedy Remove egg clusters from under leaves or remove caterpillars by hand.

MR CATERPILLAR

Encourage birds that will feed on them (see page 84). *Bacillus thuringiensis* kills only caterpillars and not the predatory insects, and is very effective when sprayed thoroughly above and below leaves.

Powdery mildew

ID A fungal disease of foliage and stems, which mostly looks as if plants have been sprinkled with white powder, on either the underside or both sides of the leaves.
Offence Stops the leaves photosynthesizing and can cause plants to die and become inedible. Attacks ornamental flowers (including begonias, dahlias, sunflower, phlox) and fruit and veg (including apples, squash and cucumber family members) from spring on.
Defence None.
Remedy Prune out any affected growth immediately and destroy. Keep plants healthy by mulching and watering. Use fungicide spray. Some gardeners recommend a solution of milk and water with around one-third milk to two-thirds water.

70
60
50
40
30
20
10
5
0

Earwig

MRS EARWIG

NATURALLY HEALTHY

Increase the diversity in your garden and natural predators will be able to pursue their vocation. If you overuse chemicals then you diminish their ability to do the job nature gave them. Keep plants healthy and they will be able to combat pests more easily. Maintain nutrient levels with compost and mulching (see page 18).

A flower and vegetable army marches on its nutrients.

Earwigs

ID Yellowish-brown insects about 2.5cm (1in) long with pincers at the rear.
Offence Eats petals and young leaves at night; loves dahlias, chrysanthemums and clematis in particular.
Defence Eats small insect pests.
Remedy Avoid providing daytime sleeping facilities to nocturnal-feeding earwigs in fences by planting flowers well away.

Place upturned plant pots on canes among the flowers, fill with scrunched-up newspaper or straw and shake out daily.

Chemical sprays are available but could damage other wildlife.

Mould (*Botrytis cinerea*)

ID A fungal disease that is grey and fuzzy-looking.
Offence Attacks many ornamentals and fruit, causing buds and flowers to shrivel and die; can cause strawberries to rot.
Remedy Remove dead or dying leaves, buds or flowers as soon as possible and destroy. Do not put in compost. Provide good air circulation around plants.

No approved fungicides.

Codling moth larvae

ID Caterpillar of the codling moth.
Offence Premature dropping of apples, pears and walnuts bored into by the maggots.
Defence Part of ecosystem.
Remedy Preventative spraying. Pheromone traps in fruit trees in early summer to lure adult male moths into the sticky trap from which exit is impossible.

REFLECTIONS ON A POND

Ponds in a small garden are visually appealing, good for reflective moments and beneficial for wildlife. Look at your sketch (see page 10), work out where best to position it, and choose between a sunken, raised or hybrid (partially in the ground) design.

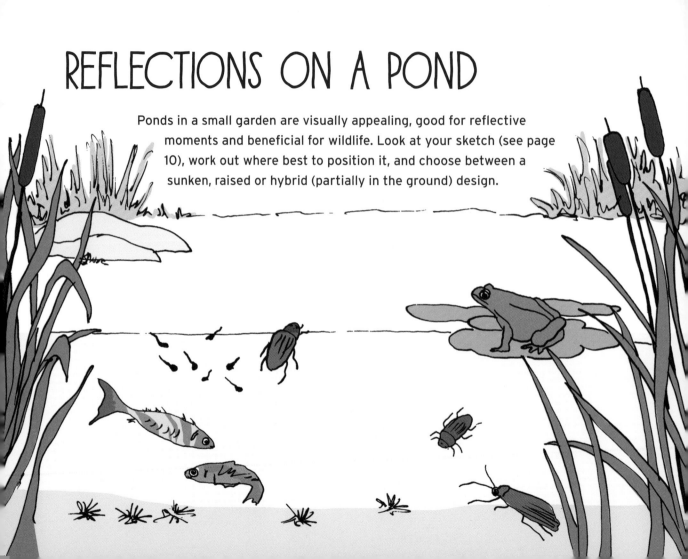

Choose a level site with lots of sun and some light shade, well away from trees that will shed unwanted leaves into the water. Wildlife such as toads and frogs find sunken ponds easier to get in and out of, but including rocks and a gentle slope up to a raised pond will give them a helping hand or foot. Raised ponds involve less effort and there are some new high-tech materials on the market along with pre-formed, pre-moulded rigid shapes. Don't forget troughs, pre-loved butcher's sinks and bathtubs or the option of lining an unusual low-cost structure, such as a pile of painted tyres, a large tractor tyre or an old wine or whisky barrel. Just check your choice is waterproof (goes without saying ...). Go micro and have a tiny pond in a simple container or birdbath, but remember it might freeze in a single block in a harsh winter so you may need to find a less exposed site. Portable ponds are on the move.

CREATING YOUR OWN POND

If you go the DIY-sunken route, make it reasonably wide and deep to make a real impression (literally) within the context of your plot. Line it with a flexible pond liner bought from hardware stores, or use thick waterproof plastic.

A healthy pond has the correct balance of plants and oxygen. Wildlife and green life can then enjoy it in equal measure. Keep the water free of dead foliage and prune your submerged plants from time to time. Fill with rainwater, if possible, as tap water contains chemicals you don't want. You can stop a pond icing over by floating an inflated ball on the surface.

Building Ideally, build and fill your pond in the winter so that it has time to settle and mature before you put anything in it. **Planting** Pond plants should ideally be a mixture of oxygenating plants (the submerged plants that produce oxygen and provide cover for wildlife) and some aquatics (surface-floating plants that keep the water cooler and discourage algae) plus a few marginals (that grow in shallower water at the edges – these plants are also good for breaking up an otherwise too-perfect pond outline). Try to go with native plants if possible, or a brawny non-native species may muscle in and take over your pond. Planting depths vary according to species, with some plants needing only a little amount of water above their crown and others needing over 30cm (12in). Select your plant size according to the dimensions of your pond and remember that they flower at different times.

Underwater Oxygenating plants – pondweed, water crowfoot, water soldier, water violet.

On the surface Aquatic plants include water hawthorn, dwarf water lily, water soldier (in small ponds it is advisable to grow in containers or aquatic baskets to prevent them from becoming too invasive, planted in garden soil or aquatic compost).

At the edge Marginals include water irises, marsh marigolds, grasses, reeds or bog plants (possibly in pots around the pond).

Keep it clean Try to keep the water as clean as possible - the plants will help.

You may want to think about installing a pump.

Pond friends Amphibians (see page 85), dragonflies, birds looking for insects and bathing opportunities, pond skaters, water beetles, ducks and moorhens (on sizeable ponds). And fish of course (although ornamental fish and heron are not natural friends).

PAVING'S THE WAY FORWARD

Paths come in many forms, casual and formal, rustic and modern. As in life, you can forge your own or follow a well-trodden one. They not only take you on a journey but they can also change the nature of the environment. It's time to be led up the garden path.

THE A TO B OF PATHS

The backbone of a garden, a path provides a practical route around the plot that prevents plant damage, divides it into different sections and directs both traffic and the eye.

Simple paving solutions include loose gravel (available in different colours), cobbles, pebbles, crushed shells, stones and bark (suitable for smaller paths among flowers). Paths made of loose material will need some edging (tiles, half-bricks or bits of slate) and you may want to put a weed-suppressant membrane under the gravel to prevent weed growth. Pebbles fixed in concrete to a design of your choice make a cheaper hybrid option. For a Zen path in Japanese tea-garden style, stepping stones are a lovely addition.

More expensive paths come in the form of slate, stone and brick.

Try to achieve harmony between path and planting and to complement your home rather than compete with it. A wide, modern geometric path in a small rural garden is like wearing a three-piece city suit at a festival. A rustic, winding path in a geometric urban garden would be like going barefoot to a board meeting. Old brick, sliced tree trunks or sawn logs, or a pebble mosaic would be a better match. Slabs of stone placed in an irregular pattern or bricks placed at angles with plants at the edge look very striking. Plants between the stones or slabs bring added interest.

THE EYES HAVE IT

If putting in a new path, go back to your sketch (see page 10), draw in some lines and mark out a potential path using lengths of rope, hosepipe or a line of trickled sand. In a long, narrow garden, a winding path that goes from side to side gives the impression of greater width.

In a wide but not very long plot, a path that narrows towards the end of the garden can make it look longer, just as placing larger objects near the house and smaller ones further away creates a sense of depth and distance.

WHAT THE DECK?

Deck dreams can be fulfilled even in the smallest space, but consider its intended use: entertaining, relaxing, eating, working? If your kitchen door opens onto an area where you could slot in a deck, make an outdoor dining room. Try to make your dream deck look organic and in context, a natural extension of the home rather than a wooden Tardis that has landed unexpectedly. It can be curved or straight, formal or informal. Attractive planted containers form low green walls and link it with the rest of the garden. Benches and tables with storage features make your deck work for its space. Think creatively and imaginatively. Plant some succulents in a container and cut a hole in your wooden deck to accommodate the planter, and you will have some interesting green areas on board.

CLEARING THE WAY

Sometimes the path to a perfect garden is littered with overgrown plants, a weed jungle, a dying lawn, and junk left by the previous owner. First step: clear the rubbish. Second step: Repair any damaged fences, fix or get fixed any unsafe walls or structures (if you are renting, this should be part of your landlord's responsibility). Third step: take some time out to think how you want your garden to look (see page 10). Go back to the sketch.

Prune Hard prune overgrown shrubs and hedges (see page 53). Think about replacing some in the longer term.

Weed Lever out weeds, preferably when the soil is moist after rain. Invasive weeds like ground elder and Japanese knotweed may have taken hold in a neglected garden and are extremely difficult to get rid of, striking terror into the heart of the new homeowner. They can be tackled organically, but you have to remove every last scrap of root. You can also weaken the plant by cutting the foliage as soon as it reappears. You may need to resort to zapping with an appropriate super-strength weedkiller or even calling in a professional contractor/eradicator. Never compost or put knotweed in household or green waste collection. (Also, see page 66.)

Make a trunk call There may be legal restrictions on removing and pruning trees (if you live in a conservation area, if the tree has a preservation order or if you are renting). Remember that trees provide privacy and protection and something to hug. Remove tree stumps.

Ditch the creepers Check for plants you would be better off ditching, including ivy and trumpet vine (choke other plants) and bamboo (runs riot). Check for things that have got out of control, such as mint (control it in containers) or *Euphorbia esula* (leafy spurge – crowds out other species). Do some research and cut them down or hand pull them. Do not put them in the compost.

Turf it If you have inherited a lawn on its last legs, you may need to start over. Try to remove it in the summer months as it will be more heavy-going in the rain. Rent or borrow a sod cutter or think about going the herbicide route. The solarisation method involves covering with black plastic sheets and newspaper, weighted with bricks, for six weeks (no peeking), after which you water and fertilize and then kill any stubborn shoots. A final mow and then up and out it goes.

If your lawn is alive but resembles a horizontal Rapunzel, use a trimmer and a mower. A good haircut will reveal what lurks beneath, which could include weeds and bald patches, mole holes and moss.

GARDEN ENEMIES

Japanese knotweed (Fallopia japonica), Himalayan balsam (Impatiens glandulifera), giant hogweed (Heracleum mantegazzianum), Australian swamp stonecrop (Crassula helmsii), parrot's feather (Myriophyllum aquaticum), floating pennywort (Hydrocotyle ranunculoides) and creeping water primrose (Ludwigia peploides).

GREEN LIVING

Lawns can be postage-stamp or plot-size. A glorious feature of country gardens, they look grassy-sassy in the city too. Emerald focal points, formal or informal in shape, they are loved by owners, wildlife (and weeds).

Small city lawns tend to look better in controlled, geometric shapes, but country equivalents can let their green hair down a bit with softer edges and sensual curves. A circular lawn pushes out the boundaries of a plot visually in all directions. If you have sufficient light for a lawn to thrive, then consider one (and where to store your mower, but mini-models are available). A compost bin is a good home for the cuttings (see page 19). Research the best seed mix or turf for your conditions.

LAWN CARE

Mowing is the hard-work bit. There are no set rules about the frequency of a lawn cut but you will need to do so quite regularly, (from weekly to more often) between spring and autumn.

FOOD AND WATER

New lawns need lots of watering, but more established ones are usually quite resilient. Feed your lawn with a high-nitrogen feed in late spring and repeat regularly until midsummer if your patch gets lots of wear and tear.

CLARIFYING SCARIFYING

There's nothing scary about scarifying. It just means regular raking to keep dead moss, grass stems and other debris under control. It also helps water and fertilizer make their way through. On a smallish lawn do this with a rake, but don't be too aggressive.

LIKING SPIKING

Lawns in small gardens tend to get compacted and prone to waterlogging as a result. Aerating (ideally after scarifying) helps the air and water move more freely around the roots. Use a garden fork to make holes and rock the fork back and forth to enlarge - ideally at intervals of around 10cm (4in) across the lawn. Fill the holes with sand. Spring is a good time to scarify/aerate, if not, autumn.

CUT AND PASTE

Cut out a damaged section of lawn with the blade of your spade and replace with a patch of new turf. Reseeding a bald patch works more successfully than for chaps. If some edges are tatty, cut the section at the edge as a square or rectangle and reposition so that the frayed edge is now on the inside and can regrow. Doesn't work for hair.

LAWN SOS

Moss can gather on a rolling lawn with annoying ease; it is the result of too little or too much water, poor drainage, insufficient sunlight, feed or aeration, or acidic soil (among other factors). If the coverage is a bit sparse or footfall too great, moss moves in.

There are a number of remedies. Scarify your lawn in the autumn, raking it with vim and vigour, or go the chemical route, using a ferrous sulphate-based proprietary product in spring or early autumn.

If yours is a new or very recent lawn installed with proper preparation, you should be mostly moss-free, but if it does appear, apply a lawn weedkiller, following the manufacturer's instructions as to how and when. Organic lawn fertilizers can help control moss.

QUICK OR SLOW

Cultivated turf gives you an instant lawn and fewer weeds, but is a more expensive route to a green swathe. It involves work: you will need to prepare your soil, clearing, digging, levelling and making the ground firm ahead of unrolling your turf. If you are going to seed (in a good way), you will need to do some research about the best seed for your conditions. Then prepare the ground too, levelling the soil, killing weeds, digging over the ground and raking in fertilizer, and then, finally, scattering the seed carefully (in late spring or early autumn). Finish by raking over the seed lightly, to cover as much as you can with soil; if the weather is dry, water it gently using a sprinkler.

EDGING YOUR BETS

Light but durable polypropylene tiles are easy to install around a lawn and can be cut to length. With their 'mowing strip' it means you can do without lawn edge trimming and mow with confidence and speed. Otherwise, there are plenty of edging options available, including log roll, stone, mini-fence, etc.

LAWN SOLUTIONS

If you are rich in lawn ambition but short on the time needed to aerate, scarify, feed and mow, then consider a few options.

Replace your fine lawn with a harder-wearing one. When planting a new lawn,

TLC OR TURF WARS

If your lawn needs reviving with TLC (tender lawn care), give it a mow on a high setting in spring and then some lawn feed. Ten days later apply a lawn weedkiller and reseed after levelling the surface. Water well and watch it grow.

If your lawn has given up the ghost, it might be time to start over. Turf out your turf in one of the following ways in the summer rather than when things get more heavy-going in the rain.

Cut it out Rent or borrow a sod cutter and remove it.

Weed it out You can use a glyphosate-based selective lawn weedkiller (zaps weeds not grass). It takes 2–3 weeks and works better if used when the grass is growing. And do make sure it's for lawns, not a general weedkiller, which will turn your green sward to brown in an instant.

Bag it Cut your lawn short, water and cover it with black plastic sheets and newspaper, weighted down with bricks; leave for six weeks (no peeking), dig out or kill any stubborn shoots. This technique is known as solarisation and is best done at sunny times (duh).

use seed or low-maintenance turf (sometimes also called multi-purpose) or one that includes micro-clovers. Clover lawns are increasingly popular, alone or mixed with grass, as they fare better in dry and hot conditions. Bees like them too.

The final green solution is an artificial lawn. You will still have to brush it regularly to keep water pools (and moss) at bay.

WILDFLOWER LAWN

Perfect for a rural garden, a wildflower lawn (see page 82) is not too tricky to grow: sow a mixture of grass and wildflower seed and cut a couple of times a year. Alternatively, herb lawns can be both pretty and fragrant, using a mixture of herbs, such as chamomile and thyme. They need good drainage and lots of sun and don't like being trodden on too much. Alpine and heather 'lawns' are options, but are more for looking at than treading on, and need hand weeding. Plant bulbs such as daffodils and crocus for extra interest, but don't mow for six weeks after flowering.

CHAPTER TWO
READY, STEADY, GROW

Here's how to dig, plant, weed and feed to get that cottage garden you've dreamed of, or revamp a sad, shady corner. From a ten-minute potter to unwind, to a hardcore propagation session, there's plenty of scope for turning your fingers green.

GROWN FREE - PROPAGATING

Plant propagation is the art of getting plants for free – well, almost. Thanks to nature's inventiveness there's a whole Kama Sutra of ways plants reproduce. It's deeply satisfying to nurture a young, green mini-me and to send it out to make its way in the big, bold world of your garden. But first you need to invest in a little basic equipment.

GENERAL

☐ Waterproof pen/pencil and labels

☐ Secateurs and knife (sharp, clean blades essential)

☐ Pots with drainage holes at bottom (around 9cm (3½in)/15cm (6in) diameter, for seeds/cuttings)

☐ Suitable compost (for seeds or cuttings)

☐ Vermiculite or perlite (aerates/holds moisture)

☐ Horticultural grit (aids drainage)

☐ Watering can with fine rose

FOR CUTTINGS

☐ Pencil (or dibber) for making holes

☐ Hormone rooting powder (helps growth, prevents rotting)

☐ Clear plastic bags and elastic bands (or propagator)

FOR SEEDS

☐ Small sieve

☐ Seed trays (optional but useful)

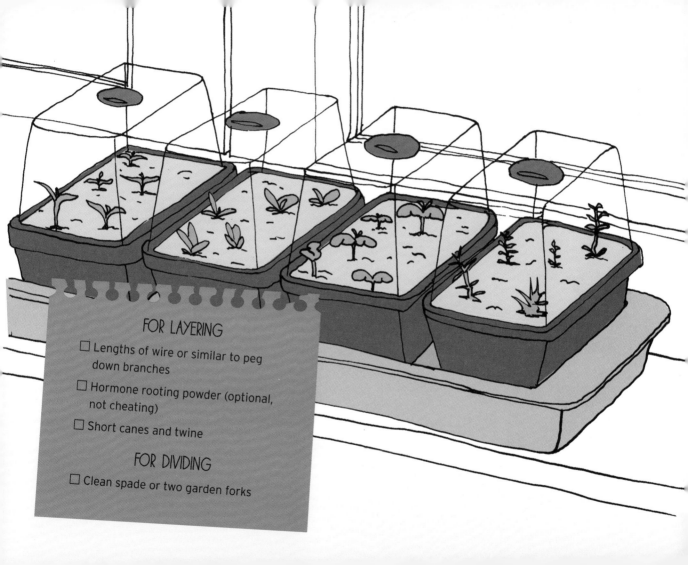

FOR LAYERING

☐ Lengths of wire or similar to peg down branches

☐ Hormone rooting powder (optional, not cheating)

☐ Short canes and twine

FOR DIVIDING

☐ Clean spade or two garden forks

SEED SCHOOL

Seeds are nature's perfect long-life packaging. Harvested at the correct time and stored in the right conditions, they can keep for years...or even centuries, as the successful germination of a 2,000-year-old date seed proved in 2005. Neanderthal nut or prehistoric pear anyone?

JURASSIC GARDEN

Buy seeds in a packet, or you can collect your own when the seed in a recently flowered plant is ripe but not yet shed. Most seed germinates best when sown soon after collecting, but that's not always possible. Packet seed has a use-by date, but if you keep your own in labelled/dated paper bags in an airtight container in a cool, dark, dry place (or even in the fridge at 5°C), it should last well. Choose a healthy plant to increase your chances of success, and collect the seed in dry conditions, or leave it to dry out if you have to collect when damp. A good tip is to place the flower head in a paper bag to avoid losing any seed when you cut if off. Clean off any bits of husk, which could carry disease or lead to the seed rotting.

Be careful to keep the roots intact when removing young plants from their trays or pots. When getting plug plants out of their modules, push them out from below using the end of a pencil.

SOW PERFECT

First you need to germinate your seeds; here's how it's done.

1 Fill a pot to the brim with seed compost and tamp it down with the base of another pot (so it's around 1cm [½ in] lower than the brim).

2 Sprinkle seeds over the compost; it helps to pour very tiny seeds into your palm and then sprinkle with thumb and finger.

3 Some seeds (lettuce, begonias) need light to germinate, so just press them down gently into the compost, or cover with a thin layer of vermiculite or perlite. Others prefer the dark (centaurea,

verbena), so sprinkle a thin layer of compost (a sieve helps) over them.

4 Water from the bottom by standing the pot in a tray of water until the top is moist.

5 Cover with a plastic bag using an elastic band (or place in a propagator).

6 For sun-worshipping seeds that like the light, put the pot in a warm spot (not direct sunlight). Not all seeds need light, so choose a warm dark place for seed goths.

7 Try to keep the seeds at an even temperature and don't let the pots dry out, watering from the bottom as before, but don't saturate.

8 When the seedlings start to emerge, remove the plastic bag/propagator, so the air circulates and they don't rot, and keep them warm and watered. Those that germinate in the dark can now be put in the light, but not direct sunlight.

SOW CAREFUL

The next stage is transplanting the seedlings to grow them on, also known as 'pricking out'; this takes place when the second set of leaves has emerged.

9 Fill trays or 15cm (6in) diameter pots with potting compost.

10 Using a pencil, carefully remove the seedlings without disturbing the roots. Handle very carefully by the leaves, not the stem.

11 Use the pencil to make holes for each seedling in the trays/pots. Lower the roots into the hole and plant the seedlings to the same depth as before, firming the soil gently around them then water (see panel, right).

12 Grow seedlings in a warm greenhouse or on a windowsill; don't let them dry out, but never saturate.

Young seedlings don't need a power shower that will flatten them instantly. A more gentle approach is to turn the rose on your watering can upside down and tilt it until the water comes out. Hold the can to one side of the pots and pass it back and forth over them several times.

A few weeks before you intend to plant them out, seedlings need to be hardened off - acclimatized to the world outside. Depending upon your local conditions, it could mean placing them in a cool spot indoors first, graduating to somewhere sheltered outside for a few hours a day, increasing the time and amount of exposure gradually.

CUTTING CLASS

One of the most popular ways of propagating is to take cuttings from stems, roots and sometimes leaves. You can't choose your parents, but you can for your young plants – look for a healthy stem or root from a healthy plant for a big bouncing baby plant, then apply TLC till it's ready for big school.

HARDWOOD CUTTINGS

- Use long, woody stems, one year old, or well-ripened stems from the current year's growth, not too thick, but no thinner than a pencil.
- Good for many deciduous plants – roses, climbers (honeysuckle, jasmine), shrubs (mock orange, viburnum, dogwood), trees; also fruit (currants, gooseberries, figs) and evergreens with broad leaves (camellia, azalea).
- Take cuttings in autumn to late winter (dormant period), after leaves have fallen and before growth starts again, but not during frost.
- The slowest cuttings to take are usually ready to transplant the following autumn.

Dig a trench around 20cm (8in) deep and dig in some compost. Hardwood cuttings can also be grown in deep pots (50:50 multi-purpose compost:coarse grit) and left somewhere sheltered outside. In very cold winters, keep in a frost-free place such as a greenhouse or cold frame. In summer, ensure the cuttings don't dry out. You can also dig some compost into the soil and plant directly where the cutting is to grow, but protect during frost.

Cut your chosen stem into sections of around 20–25cm (8–10in); take several cuttings in case not

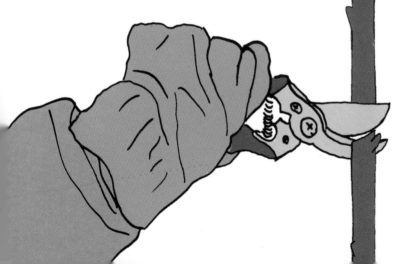

all are successful. Cut off the bottom of each section below a bud/pair of buds (horizontally across the stem), then cut off the top of the section just above another bud (a sloping cut, so water will run off; see image). Remove any side shoots and leaves. Using a knife, wound each cutting at the base. Dip the base in hormone rooting powder. Insert the cuttings in the trench, spaced about 10-15cm (4-6in) apart, and then fill in the soil around them. Around two-thirds of each cutting should be below the surface. Root less hardy plants (cistus, hibiscus) in pots in a frost-free greenhouse.

SEMI-RIPE (SEMI-HARDWOOD) CUTTINGS

 Use stems from the current season's growth, firm but with a soft tip.

 Good for evergreen shrubs (mahonia, berberis), trees (holly, magnolia), hardy climbers (solanum, passion flower), hedging (box, privet, laurel), groundcover plants (periwinkle, creeping raspberry), herbs (rosemary, lavender, bay).

 Take cuttings midsummer-early autumn; best in the morning to avoid wilting.

 Roots usually develop in 6-10 weeks, several months if taken in autumn.

Fill some pots 9cm (3½in) in diameter for single cuttings, 15cm (6in) for several. Don't allow the leaves to touch) with 50:50 potting compost and perlite/vermiculite. Cut a 15-20cm (6-8in) section from the tip of your chosen stem. Cut off the tip just above a leaf; at the base, cut across just below a leaf. Cut off the leaves and side shoots from the lower part of the stem, leaving three or four leaves at the top. Make a hole in the compost with a pencil, dip the base of the cutting in hormone rooting powder and insert the stem up to the lowest leaves. Firm the compost around the cutting, then water. Cover the pot with a plastic bag, held with an elastic band (don't allow the bag to touch the leaves - sticks placed at the side will help), or place in a propagator. Keep in a frost-free place and remove the cover a couple of times a week for 15 minutes or so to ventilate; don't allow the soil to dry out. Pot on when healthy root systems have developed and harden off before planting out (see page 41).

Like a pale townie, fresh off the plane with a bottle of factor 50, semi-ripe and softwood cuttings soon wilt in the sun. Place them in a plastic bag in the shade as soon as they are cut - ideally deal with straight away. Otherwise, place the bag in a fridge, but deal with in less than 12 hours.

SOFTWOOD CUTTINGS

 Use tips of non-flowering soft, new growth.

 Good for tender and hardy perennials, deciduous shrubs (hydrangea, fuchsia).

 Take cuttings in spring–early summer, early morning to avoid wilting.

 Roots usually develop in 6–10 weeks.

Fill some pots with compost as for semi-ripe cuttings. Cut about a 10cm (4in) section from the tip of your chosen stem. Pinch out the soft tip, then trim the base just below a leaf joint and cut off the leaves on the lower part of the cutting, leaving two or three at the top. Dip the base in hormone rooting powder and insert the stem into the compost to around half its length. Insert several cuttings around the edge of the pot (leaves must not touch each other) and firm the compost around them. Water, then cover with a plastic bag held in place with an elastic band (don't allow the bag to touch the leaves; sticks placed at the side will help) or propagator. Keep in a warm position, such as a windowsill, but not in direct sunlight and keep the compost moist (watering from below). Remove the cover a couple of times a week for 15 minutes or so. Pot on when healthy root systems have developed and harden off before planting out (see page 41).

AND THERE'S MORE

There are still more ways of taking cuttings, including heel cuttings (woody stems) - hold a side shoot and pull it away and down so that a piece of stem comes off with it. Proceed as for semi-ripe cuttings. Or use a whole leaf with its stalk, or cut across a leaf and place the cut section in compost (good for houseplants).

ROOT CUTTINGS

 Usually taken in winter when the plant is dormant and generally produce good results.

 Ideally choose roots that are no thicker than a pencil.

Fill a tray or pot with cuttings compost, water well and allow to drain. Small plants can be dug out to access the roots; dig down beside large plants *in situ* and scrape away soil from the roots. Choose a strong root and cut if off near the top (horizontally and remember that's the top). Cut into sections of 5-12cm (2-4¾in). Use a horizontal cut at the top and a slanted cut at the bottom.

For thick roots, make a hole in the compost and insert the cutting (right way up) so the top is level with the surface.

For thin roots, lay the cutting horizontally and cover with 2-3cm (about 1in) of compost. Depending on the plant's hardiness, keep in a warm (windowsill) or frost-free place. Water minimally but don't allow to dry out. Pot on when a good root system has developed.

PROPAGATION INSPIRATION

If you find you have a proper knack for propagation, here are some more ideas to kick-start your plant stock.

BULBS

Many bulbs increase by forming small mini-bulbs (offsets) around the base of the parent. In spring, before active growth begins, dig up a clump and gently rock and twist off the offsets from the parent.

Pot up small offsets now to plant out a season or two later, or plant out larger ones directly. They will generally take a few years to start flowering. You can also detach offsets when lifting bulbs for storage (see page 56).

It's a good idea to separate bulb clumps every couple of years anyway to avoid overcrowding.

Bulbs can also be grown from seed, but won't flower for a number of years – buying new bulbs is quicker.

Some plants, such as alpines, produce entire young plants beside the parent. Pull them off gently or separate them with a sharp knife.

LAYERING

Use non-flowering stems that can be bent down to the ground.

 Good for many climbers (ivy, honeysuckle), deciduous shrubs (lilac, wisteria) and is a handy way of thickening up a hedge. Some climbers are expensive so it makes financial sense too.

 Layer in spring or autumn.

 Roots usually develop within two seasons.

About 30cm (12in) from the stem tip, at a point where a leaf emerges from the stem, make a slanting cut (no deeper than half the stem width) through the underside of the stem. Remove the leaf and any others on the part of the stem that will be in contact with the soil. Apply a little hormone rooting powder to the cut (if using). Press the cut side down into the soil, peg in position (with bent wire, for example) and water well. A stone placed on top will help retain moisture. Bend the free end of the stem upwards and tie to a short cane pushed into the soil. Keep well watered. When leaves and a healthy root system have developed, your new plant is ready to leave home; cut it off from the parent and transplant.

DIVISION

 Good for perennials.

 Divide in spring for late-summer/autumn flowering plants; autumn for spring/early summer flowering.

Divide A good way of propagating or rejuvenating a mature plant, or one that's just got too big for its boots.

Water the plant a few hours before you divide it. Prepare the new location by digging in some compost or well-rotted manure. Dig out the plant with a fork. Some can be pulled apart by hand; if not, use two forks inserted back to back, or cut down through it with a spade. Make sure each smaller clump has good roots, discard any old or diseased parts. Remove the roots of any entangled weeds before replanting to the same depth as before (as soon as possible, before the roots dry out) and water well.

USES FOR MINI-GREENHOUSES

Start seeds/grow on seedlings

Grow on cuttings/ young plants

Harden off tender young plants (see page 41)

Provide extra warmth for fruit and veg in a cold spell

Extend growing season/encourage quicker ripening of fruit and veg

Overwinter/shield tender plants from wind and rain

MINI-GREENHOUSE RULES

You might be lucky enough to inherit or have space for a 'proper' greenhouse, but if not, mini-greenhouses and cold frames are great alternatives.

They have the advantage of being moveable feasts (literally, if you are growing fruit and veg), which can be repositioned for light or shade. If you enjoy potting, not to mention pottering, you are unlikely to regret a modest investment in one of these.

SITING YOUR GREENHOUSE

Ranging from deluxe walk-in to petite lean-to, the most common mini-greenhouses consist of a loose plastic cover over a frame with shelving. Higher rise than a cold frame, they take up less valuable floor space, but the vertical shelving can also create shade, so bear in mind that the top shelf is the sunniest. Position for maximum light but watch out for wind – a sharp gust could send it shooting off, drone-like, to land in a neighbour's garden and scare the children/dog/gnomes. Positioned against a wall (lean-tos are specifically designed for this), they are less exposed to wind.

COLD FRAMES

A simple square/rectangular frame, with a sloping transparent lid of rigid plastic/glass that can be propped open for ventilation. Sides made of brick or wood offer the best protection from the cold, but many are made of polycarbonate. Lightweight frames can be moved around easily to follow the sun. Or improvise and make your own from recycled materials – an old window frame placed on top of a couple of drawers – keep an eye on those skips. Position in full sun if possible, on a base that provides drainage. Dig in some compost and grow plants directly in the soil, or lay a base of gravel. If the base is solid (such as paving), pots can be placed in trays.

VENTILATION

Allowing air to circulate to prevent the build-up of moisture (leading to disease/rotting) is essential. So make the most of lids, vents and zips, unless the conditions are positively monsoon or Arctic.

SCORCHIO OR COOLIO

In winter, you can't just relax on the sofa with a glass of Chianti and a TV box set thinking your plants are equally snuggly tucked up in their greenhouse or cold frame. Unlike sophisticated greenhouses that can be heated, frost can penetrate a more modest installation. Line the inside with a layer of bubble wrap (the downside is that it reduces light). Positioning against the wall of a house also helps.

In summer, beware of overheating and scorching foliage, so remember to remove any extra insulation and even think about shading. An old curtain or blind draped over a mini-greenhouse can be raised/lowered as necessary. Shading washes are also available – they are painted on but have to be washed off for winter. Alternatively, flexible mesh sold on a roll can be cut to length and allows some light through.

FLOWERS AND FOLIAGE

Whether you grow them for their flowers or their leaves, the huge range of plants available means there will always be something interesting to look at in your garden.

FLOWERS

Many plants are grown for their flowers, produced at some time between spring and the first frosts, though a few tough it out in winter (pansy, bergenia, hellebore).

 Annuals (nasturtium, cosmos, busy lizzy) are grown fresh each year. They produce a colourful show fairly quickly and are good for filling gaps.

 Biennials (foxglove, see panel opposite) have a two-year life cycle, usually flowering in the second year.

Perennials live for three years or more and can largely be left to their own devices. Many are herbaceous perennials, which die back in autumn to do a boy band-style comeback the following year.

 There's also a wide range of flowering shrubs (see page 52), ornamental trees (see page 54) and climbers (see page 59) that add to the general bloom fest.

FOLIAGE

Plants are also grown for their attractive foliage (coleus, brunnera, angelica, heuchera, hosta, castor oil plant, astilbe, phormium, Persian shield, ferns, caladium or elephant ear, ligularia and canna lily), although many do the double and have attractive flowers, too. Not forgetting succulents (aloe, houseleek and echeveria) if conditions permit, and a whole range of ornamental grasses and shrubs (see the following pages).

Some perennials are grown as annuals, but few plants are true biennials; for example, the hollyhock is a short-lived perennial treated as a biennial. Many plants have both annual and perennial varieties.

HOW TO GROW THEM

Plant (or sow, see page 40) annuals, biennials and perennials in weeded, forked and raked over soil in an open, sunny site. Shepherd tender biennials into their second year under the protection of a cloche or horticultural fleece in winter. Follow packet instructions if sowing where seeds are to grow, and cover with netting or twigs to keep cats/birds away. Water carefully using a fine rose (see page 41). Remove the weakest seedlings to thin them out, and water regularly until established.

Perennials are normally around for a long time, so take note of spread/ height at maturity and be choosy about position (location, location, location! – though they can be moved, see page 61). Plant in spring or autumn (see page 60). In spring, before new growth starts, cut back old stems/ leaves to ground level on deciduous perennials, leaving any new growth that has already come through at the base. Most healthy evergreen perennials can be left as is, or can just be tidied up.

BEDDING

Annual and biennial bedding plants are sold in multi-packs or as plug plants (seedlings) in spring, ready to plant out directly in borders and containers, not to mention parks and a thousand municipal planting schemes across the country. They look very tempting, but don't buy too soon as they shouldn't be planted until all risk of frost is past. You could be left with trays of plants that need sheltering or even growing on under cover until it's safe for them to venture out. Winter bedding (viola, cyclamen) is available, too, so it's possible to have a more or less continuous display. When you have more green fingers and space, raise your own bedding from seed; most is quick and easy to grow (see page 40).

SHRUBS

Shrubs are low-maintenance woody plants (deciduous and evergreen). Use them to give structure and year-round interest, as a backdrop to annuals and perennials, in hedging, or plant a whole border of shrubs or a single shrub as a specimen.

LOOKING AFTER YOUR SHRUBS

🌿 Water new shrubs regularly until established; mature shrubs normally don't need much watering, apart from in periods of extended drought (see page 60).

🌿 Once a year, in early spring, a slow-release fertilizer can be applied (see page 64), followed by a mulch (see page 65). Cut off suckers (see panel, opposite left) as close as possible to the plant (or rub off if the sucker is small enough).

🌿 Flowering shrubs include rhododendron, azalea, elderberry, ceanothus, rosemary, rock rose, heather, lavatera, potentilla and St John's wort (see also page 73).

🌿 Shrubs grown primarily for their foliage include ninebark, smoke bush, barberry, deutzia, hebe, winter creeper, choisya, spiraea, holly, dogwood (colourful stems) and santolina.

🌿 Some shrubs can't decide whether to major on fantastic foliage or flowers: pieris has fiery-red leaves and lovely white or pink flowers in spring, as does the pink-flowering Chinese fringe flower.

🌿 Small shrubs can be grown in loam-based compost in containers. Use topiary/specimen shrubs as features in a formal garden (see page 76).

🌿 Tender shrubs grown in containers can be whisked away to a sheltered spot when the weather turns biblical (palms, oleander). Water regularly and feed as necessary. Top-dress every year – replace the top 5–10cm (2–4in) of compost with fresh. Water and apply a mulch of bark chippings/gravel. Repot every 2–3 years, renewing the compost completely. Prune out dead stems. If the roots are very congested, tease them out with a fork. If keeping in the same pot, the roots can be pruned by up to two-thirds.

HEDGES

As well as marking boundaries, hedges can be used as windbreaks (see page 62) and to divide up a plot (see page 76). If planting from scratch, buy more plants than you need in case some don't survive and you need to plug a gap.

Deciduous or evergreen? Deciduous hedges filter strong winter winds rather than create turbulence with a solid barrier, evergreens soften traffic noise all year (and thorns deter burglars and next door's cat). Clip formal hedges to maintain shape and restrict height: privet twice a year, spring/late summer; yew late summer. Prune informal hedges to tidy them up. You may need to cut back some stems by one-third to keep the hedge thick. In snowy areas, clip the tops to a point so the weight of settled snow causes less damage.

When is a shrub a tree? Trees can be defined as woody plants with a single stem, and shrubs as woody plants with several stems. But exceptions and variations in height mean the boundaries are distinctly blurred.

Suckers are shoots that grow from a plant's roots or - on grafted plants - shoots that grow from below the graft union (see page 58). They divert energy away from the main growth, so they get the chop.

Ornamental trees grown for their attractive foliage or flowers include Japanese maple, laburnum, mimosa, magnolia, robinia, ornamental cherry/almond/plum and amelanchier.

TREES

Trees add structure and create a focal point in a garden. Flowering periods are normally short so they are grown more for their foliage or fruit, with attractive bark an added bonus. A tree large enough for Tarzan to swing past on a creeper would look out of place in a small garden, but they come in all sizes and can be grown in containers, as well.

SITING

Choose a prospective site carefully. Look at height/spread at maturity – even if it's slow growing your tiny sapling might ultimately turn into a beanstalk. Think about the shade it will cast and whether it will dominate or obstruct a view. Look at its changing colour and shape through the seasons.

PLANTING

Plant bare-root trees autumn/winter, and container-grown trees at any time, but never when the ground is frozen. Make sure the planting hole is 2–3 times wider than the root ball and loosen the soil at the bottom of the hole. Follow the planting instructions on page 60. Stake the tree securely – 'plant' the stake in the hole first, then the tree (to not damage the roots when driving in the stake). Water really well and mulch around – but not touching – the trunk. In a very windy position, use two stakes, one on either side, securing each to the trunk individually.

CARING FOR TREES

For the first 2–3 years, water well (around eight watering cans full a week in hot, dry spells). In spring apply a liquid fertilizer and mulch around the trunk. Loosen ties as the tree grows. Remove weeds around the roots and cut off any suckers at the base (see page 53).

Mature trees seldom need watering, apart from in periods of drought, but can be fed occasionally.

POT LUCK

Choose a tree suitable for a container - dwarf varieties of Japanese maple, bay tree, citrus, olive and patio fruit trees work well. Use a container at least 1½ times the depth of the root ball and around one-quarter of the tree's height or width. Add a layer of gravel or broken pots at the bottom and fill with loam-based compost mixed with a slow-release fertilizer. Insert a stake before planting. Plant at the correct depth (see page 60) and firm up the soil: it should be around 5cm (2in) below the rim. Water well and mulch with a 3cm (about 1in) layer of gravel or grit. Stand the pot on blocks for drainage. The soil in containers dries out quickly, so keep well watered (up to twice a day in hot weather). Top-dress in spring: remove any mulch and replace the top 5–6cm (about 2in) with fresh compost mixed with slow-release fertilizer; restore or add fresh mulch. Cut out any dead or diseased branches. Repot every two or three years in a larger pot, or trim the roots by up to one-third and put back into the same pot with fresh compost.

Tree roots can extend up to three times the height of the tree and can cause subsidence if positioned too near a building, or can damage drains, paths, etc. So think twice about that giant redwood – check before you buy.

GRASSES AND BULBS

Grasses add colour (not just shades of green, but silver, gold, bronze, red, even purple), structure, texture (fronds and flower heads) and movement (swaying in the wind), while bulbs will surprise you throughout the year and are among the first plants that tell you that spring is on the way.

ORNAMENTAL GRASSES

From low-growing and compact to statuesque and elegant, with long, arching stems, some grasses have a clumping habit (miscanthus, fescue, fountain grasses), while others spread (some varieties of calamagrostis and carex) and can be invasive. Bamboo is a notable culprit but can be contained by sinking a special barrier around it.

Plant among other plants, in drifts for a natural feel, or an eye-catching variety as a specimen, in spring or autumn (see page 60). Most like a sunny position in well-drained soil. They look good in containers, too (see page 98) and taller grasses can be used as a screen. They generally don't need that much attention and not that much watering once established. In early spring, before new growth starts, trim/rake out tatty leaves from evergreen grasses, but cut deciduous grasses, which turn straw-coloured, down to the ground.

BULBS

This group includes any plant that stashes its food supply, hamster-like, in a storage organ underground. Other forms include corms, tubers and rhizomes. Usually easy to grow, most bulbs flower early spring to late autumn. Pick firm, plump, blemish-free bulbs and plant when dormant: summer-flowering bulbs in spring, spring-flowering in autumn. Most like free-draining soil, so if yours doesn't fit the bill try growing them in pots.

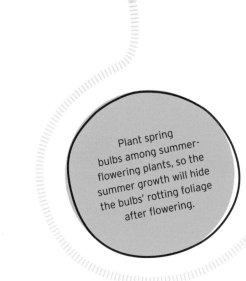

Plant spring bulbs among summer-flowering plants, so the summer growth will hide the bulbs' rotting foliage after flowering.

How to grow bulbs

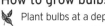 Plant bulbs at a depth of two to three times the height of the bulb (tulips 3-4 times). Space them 2-3 times their width apart. As a rule, plant with the tips upwards. If you're worried about animals digging them up, cover with wire mesh.

 To plant in grass, scatter randomly and plant where they fall. Remove plugs of turf with a bulb planter, place the bulb in the hole, cover with soil and replace the top part of the plug. Or cut an H shape in the turf and peel the two sides back. Plant the bulbs at the correct depth, cover with soil and close the 'window'.

 Like a festival-goer on the way home after several days of mud and music, bulbs don't look their best once they have flowered. But it's important to leave the foliage to rot (don't knot the leaves) for a minimum of six weeks, so nutrients can be stored in the bulb for next year.

Lifting bulbs

Once the foliage has rotted, bulbs can be dug up and stored until the following year. Snip off any remaining leaves, trim the roots and remove any flaking outer layer. Brush off the soil and place on a tray for a day or so to dry. Store in paper bags (not plastic) somewhere cool and dry. Discard any diseased bulbs. It's also a good time to propagate by dividing bulb clumps (see page 46).

ROSES AND CLIMBERS

Roses are the quintessential British flower and offer the bonus that many varieties flower more than once during the year. Climbers, such as wisteria and clematis have exquisite flowers and work well in small gardens.

Many roses are grafted. The top of the plant is grafted onto a different rose rootstock that is more hardy. The bulge at the base of the stem where the plants were joined is called the graft/bud union.

ROSES

From groundcover to tall shrub and rambling, a rose bed of choice awaits.

☑ **Hybrid tea** Bush rose, one large, single flower per stem; most repeat-flower.

☑ **Floribunda** Bush rose, flowers in clusters; flower once or repeat.

☑ **Shrub** Usually larger than bush roses with thornier stems; flower once or repeat, usually in clusters.

☑ **Climbers** Stiff stems, single flowers or in clusters; repeat-flower.

☑ **Ramblers** Long, flexible stems; flower once in summer.

☑ **Groundcover** Low-growing, many stems; flower profusely.

Most roses like sun all day. Plant bare-root roses late autumn or early spring; container-grown roses at almost any time, except when the ground is frozen.

Planting

Fork some well-rotted manure or compost mixed with bonemeal into the bottom of the planting hole. Plant so the graft union (see panel above) is 2.5cm (1in) below soil level. Otherwise, follow the instructions on page 60 but do not mulch until the next spring. Keep well watered during the first few months, particularly if the conditions are dry. To avoid rose sickness, don't plant a rose where one has been grown before.

If you've no alternative, remove the old soil and replace it with fresh.

Thanks to their deep roots, mature roses don't normally need much watering, apart from in dry periods; feed and mulch in spring. Deadhead blooms (see page 73, unless you want to preserve the hips). Watch out for mildew and black spot (see pages 21-22), which many are subject to.

CLIMBERS

Upwardly mobile climbers soften walls, adding height and interest without too much land grab. Perennial climbers (climbing hydrangea, passion flower) need pruning, while annuals (moonflower, morning glory) can be used to fill gaps quickly. They generally like their feet in the shade and their heads in the sun - shade the base with other plants.

Climbers have their equipment built in. Twiners (sweet peas, clematis) have thin flexible tendrils that wrap around their support. Stem twiners (wisteria, honeysuckle) wind their stems around instead. Those with thorns (roses, brambles) use them to hoist themselves along, while others use the roots that grow along their stems (ivy) or adhesive pads (Virginia creeper) to cling directly to walls and fencing, but can cause damage. Supports range from obelisks and wigwams, to trellis or a network of taut wires fixed to a wall or fence. Or grow a climber up through a tree. Plant at any time of year, as long as the ground is not waterlogged or frozen.

Planting climbers against a wall or fence

Install the support first. The soil close to a wall or fence is often dry so plant 35-45cm (13¾-17¾in) away (see page 60). Use canes leaning at an angle to guide young plants towards the support. Water well and mulch around the plant (see page 65). Plant clematis 5-6cm (about 2in) deeper than its original container. If training a plant up an obelisk or wigwam, dig the soil first, then erect the support. Tie in stems as the plant grows.

PLANTING PERENNIALS AND SHRUBS

Shrubs and perennials form the backbone of a garden. Many perennials die off at the end of each growing season, but will come back the following year.

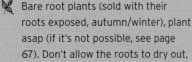 Bare root plants (sold with their roots exposed, autumn/winter), plant asap (if it's not possible, see page 67). Don't allow the roots to dry out, soak them in a bucket of water for 20 minutes before planting.

Container-grown plants can be planted at almost any time, though spring and autumn are ideal. Soak the container in a bucket of water for an hour or so before planting, and allow to drain. Remove the top layer of compost from around the plant to get rid of any moss or weeds. (See roses, page 58; trees, page 54.)

Choose a position that allows room for spread/height at maturity. Dig a hole at least twice the width of the root ball and deeper. Loosen the soil in the bottom and dig in some compost and fertilizer (see page 64).

Insert the plant in the hole, making sure it is at the same depth as it was in its pot (or the same level as before, if transplanting). Lay a cane across the hole so you can line up with the surface easily. For bare-root plants, look for a mark on the stem to show where the soil was before, or plant so the point where the stem joins the roots is level with the soil.

Gently tease out densely packed roots and spread them out in the hole. Fill in with soil all around the plant and make sure it's straight. Hold the base of the stem and wiggle it a bit to settle it in the soil, adding more if needed. Firm the soil around the plant - the traditional way is with your foot. Water well (even if rain is expected). Add a 5cm

(2in) layer of compost as a mulch (see page 65), but don't allow it to touch the stem.

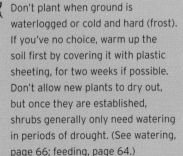 Don't plant when ground is waterlogged or cold and hard (frost). If you've no choice, warm up the soil first by covering it with plastic sheeting, for two weeks if possible. Don't allow new plants to dry out, but once they are established, shrubs generally only need watering in periods of drought. (See watering, page 66; feeding, page 64.)

MOVING SHRUBS AND PERENNIALS

Move in spring or autumn (but not when in flower), when the weather is cool but the ground not frozen. Move evergreen shrubs in spring, just before new growth starts, deciduous in autumn. Draw a circle in the soil around the shrub to the width of the plant (this usually equals the spread of the roots underground). Dig a trench around the circle, loosen the soil with a fork, and dig down and under the root ball to lift the plant out. Keep as much of the root ball as you can, but you might need to cut through woody/strong roots with secateurs. You might need a hand for a big shrub. Tilt the shrub to one side, drag a piece of plastic sheeting under it, tilt it the other way and pull the sheeting right underneath. Then it can be carried between you.

GROWING FRUIT AND VEG

Grow your own to save money, eat super-fresh food that is free of pesticides and ripened naturally, reduce your food miles to zero and, quite literally, have the pick of the crop.

TIPS FOR AN EDIBLE FEAST

Choose a sheltered, sunny spot for your kitchen garden. High winds reduce the number of pollinating insects, so plant a screen (see page 106) or hedge if it's exposed.

Grow the fruit and veg you love or that are expensive to buy.

Rich, healthy soil is essential, so dig in or mulch (see page 65) with well-rotted manure or compost every year before the planting season.

Use containers if your garden is small or to extend your edible possibilities (see page 96); choose dwarf varieties.

Keep plots weeded and keep a regular watch out for pests and diseases (see page 20).

Feed for productivity (see page 64).

Use a raised bed, mini-greenhouse/cold frame (see page 49) to start crops early.

Protect crops from birds, rabbits, etc. with netting, fleece, cages, etc.

Save time by going no-dig. Spread compost on the soil in the autumn and leave it; the worms in healthy soil will incorporate the compost into the soil for you. A quick turn with a fork in the spring is often sufficient to combine the rest before planting.

Raised beds are useful if your soil is not up to scratch – you can make it as rich, fertile and well drained as you want. Buy a kit or make your own raised bed using treated wood. Position in a sunny sheltered site. Soil warms up more quickly in raised beds so you can start crops earlier. Make them narrow enough to reach the centre from the sides. If you build one on a hard surface, make it at least 45cm (17¾ in) deep.

VEG

🌱 Sow crops like lettuce and radishes little and often (every two weeks) to keep a fresh supply going.

🌱 Unlike fruit, most veg are grown as annuals. If you don't have the time to replant every year, grow perennials, such as Jerusalem artichokes, asparagus, sorrel and watercress. Other veg usually grown as an annual but can be perennial include kale, radicchio, garlic.

🌱 Easy veg includes salad leaf, potatoes, tomatoes, beans, courgettes and asparagus (a perennial).

🌱 Make the most of a small space by planting quick-growing veg (salad leaf, radish, rocket, spring onions and carrot) between slower-growing; harvest the former before the latter has matured and spread.

FRUIT

🌱 Easy fruit includes strawberries, currants (red/white/black), raspberries, apples, rhubarb, blueberries (in ericaceous soil, see page 17), gooseberries, figs.

🌱 For a small garden choose fruit trees with dwarf (M9) or very dwarf (M27, good for containers) rootstock.

🌱 Thin out to improve the quality and size of fruit, for example thin dessert apples to one or two every 10-15cm (4-6in), or one per cluster.

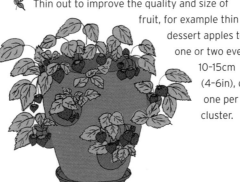

HERBS

Growing herbs from seed (see page 40) is the cheapest way of obtaining annual herbs. Grow them on in a sunny position in free-draining soil. Pick regularly to keep the plants producing leaves, and remove flowers from herbs grown for foliage (chives, mint). Prune woody herbs (thyme, rosemary) after flowering. Grow mint in a container, to control its spread.

FEED ME!

Fertilizer comes in liquid, powder, pellet or granule form and is inorganic (manufactured) or organic.

Organic types include blood, fish, bonemeal, chicken manure pellets and seaweed-based. Or make your own by steeping nettle or comfrey leaves in water for several weeks – in a container with a lid as it smells. Use it diluted. Feed plants to improve growth and to produce more fruit/blooms. Fast-growing and highly productive plants in particular (rhubarb, tomatoes) benefit from fertilizer. It also helps correct nutrient deficiency (yellow leaves, stunted growth). Some are specially formulated, such as for lawns or roses, while tomato fertilizer can be used on

FERTILIZER TYPES

Slow-release Applied as a powder to the soil around a plant; must not touch leaves. Usually in spring, often used on lawns.

Controlled release Granules added to soil when planting, good for containers. (Use liquid feed for fruit and veg in containers.)

Liquid feed/water-soluble Watered onto the roots (not foliage), fast-acting, good for fruit and veg and to correct nutrient deficiency. Foliar feeding (a dilute solution watered onto leaves) is also good for nutrient deficiency and for supplementary feeding.

Lime or lime-rich material (such as mushroom compost) Helps improve veg yields. Spread on the soil (follow packet instructions), but don't plant for a least a month.

Green manure Certain plants (alfalfa, mustard, crimson clover, etc.) are grown *in situ* to dig back into the soil 2-3 months later to enrich it. Usually sown in autumn on the ground that's not being used. Also helps to prevent soil erosion and suppress weeds.

any fast-growing fruit/veg. Use in spring/summer during the growing season, as per the packet instructions. For plants grown in normal, fertile soil in beds and borders there is often no need to add fertilizer. Don't overfeed, it can be just as bad as not feeding, leading to wilting or even killing the plant.

Mulching (see below) or digging in well-rotted organic matter (garden compost, manure) is a way of feeding via the soil, as it helps build up soil fertility over time. If you mulch, it's not always necessary to feed plants, too.

If slugs have moved into your organic mulch, remove it in spring, leave the soil exposed for a few weeks, then replace with fresh. This will help to eliminate slugs, snails and their offspring, who packed their bags to overwinter among it.

Watch out when using fertilizer, particularly the chemical sort – wash your hands afterwards and don't breathe in any dust.

MULCHING

The gentle art of spreading a layer of material over the soil, helping it to retain moisture and keep warm, and to suppress weeds by cutting off the light they need to germinate. Organic mulch also helps to build up soil fertility and improve its structure.

Mulch beds and borders once a year, mid-late spring. Clear all weeds and water well first. Use inorganic mulch in a layer 2.5–5cm (1–2in) thick; it includes gravel, geotextile membranes that you can plant through (see page 79) and black plastic sheeting (camouflaged by bark or gravel. Use organic mulch in a layer 5–10cm (2–4in) thick (avoid touching the plants); it includes well-rotted manure, garden compost, leaf mould and chipped bark.

EAU SO IMPORTANT

Established plants with good root systems normally don't need watering every day, even when it's hot (unless visibly wilting), but new plants do – water after planting and daily until they're established. Those in the know have lots of watery top tips – here are some more.

WATERING TIPS

- Watering thoroughly and less frequently is better than little and often. Soaking the soil encourages roots to grow down, whereas a light sprinkling may evaporate before it can penetrate the soil, encouraging thirsty roots to remain closer to the surface.
- Water fruit and veg well when the plants are flowering and developing edible parts.
- Water plants in containers and hanging baskets daily in warm weather or even twice a day. Water-retaining gel can be added to the compost or to the soil around specific plants in borders. (For watering seeds/seedlings, see page 41.)
- Water the soil rather than the plants, early morning or late evening when it's cooler (unless the local slugs and snails party at night big-time), to reduce evaporation.
- To make sure water soaks into the soil around a plant – particularly on a sloping site – build a small ridge around the plant.
- Invest in an automatic watering system. They include sprinklers and seep/trickle hoses containing small holes that are laid between plants and can be operated on timers.

ECO-FRIENDLY

Install a water butt to catch rainfall. Mulching (see page 65) helps to retain moisture, as does digging in garden compost or well-rotted manure. Dense planting means less water evaporation as less soil is exposed, but dig out weeds that compete for water. Avoid digging during dry periods as moist soil from lower levels will be brought to the surface and dry out.

WEED WORKS

Weeds are just plants in the wrong place, or so they say, but pernicious weeds (ground elder, bindweed) are the raptors of the weed world, designed to terrorize and turn your garden Jurassic with their long entwining roots. Strike early before they can flower and set seed. The choices are: annual weeds – dig them out, hoe seedlings so they dry and die on the surface, spray with weedkiller; perennials – dig out (but they can regrow from the tiniest scrap of root left behind), blast with a flame gun, zap with a glysophate weedkiller, suppress with plastic sheeting or a mulch (see page 65).

ROOTING FOR YOU

Roots absorb water and nutrients from the soil, and keep plants safely anchored if conditions turn Biblical. The head honcho is the tap root, a long, prominent root (wider at the top, may have smaller roots branching off it) that works its way down through the soil. Plants with deep tap roots have greater tolerance to drought but are difficult to dig out. Fibrous roots are more shallow, multiple roots of around the same size. Some plants have a combination of the two.

HEELING IN

If you can't plant out immediately, dig a trench (in a sheltered position in winter, in the shade in summer) big enough to take your plants' roots/root ball. Lay them down so the roots are in the trench, cover well with soil and keep watered.

NIPPING IT IN THE BUD

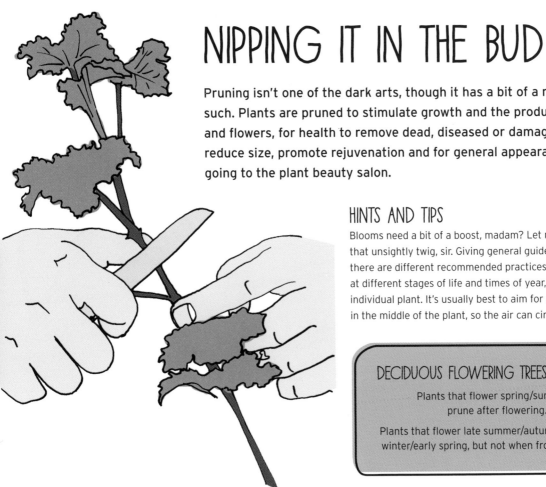

Pruning isn't one of the dark arts, though it has a bit of a reputation as such. Plants are pruned to stimulate growth and the production of fruit and flowers, for health to remove dead, diseased or damaged stems, to reduce size, promote rejuvenation and for general appearance - a bit like going to the plant beauty salon.

HINTS AND TIPS

Blooms need a bit of a boost, madam? Let me help you with that unsightly twig, sir. Giving general guidelines is tricky as there are different recommended practices for different plants at different stages of life and times of year, so check for your individual plant. It's usually best to aim for an open framework in the middle of the plant, so the air can circulate.

DECIDUOUS FLOWERING TREES AND SHRUBS

Plants that flower spring/summer - prune after flowering.

Plants that flower late summer/autumn - prune late winter/early spring, but not when frost is expected.

🌿 Use secateurs, loppers or shears with sharp, clean blades to minimize the chances of disease getting into the plant at the point where it is cut/wounded. A pruning saw with a pointed end is useful for getting between thicker branches.

🌿 Not everything needs full-on pruning, sometimes just an occasional trim and tidy-up will do, but some plants do benefit from being pruned annually. For example, it's important to prune fruit trees and bushes, so they keep on producing good crops of fruit.

🌿 Plants respond differently to pruning according to the time of year – on a flowering shrub, shortening young, green stems in spring stimulates side growth. Shortening the same stems in summer, when they are more mature, encourages flower buds. Shortening the stems in winter produces vigorous growth in spring. Hard pruning in early spring (cutting back severely) promotes vigorous growth.

🌿 To shorten a stem, cut it back to just above a bud; this will stimulate the bud to grow out in the direction it is facing. On stems with buds arranged alternately, make a slanting cut (see image, page 42) above a bud. The usual advice is to pick an outward-facing bud, so the centre of the plant doesn't become congested. Slant the cut so water runs down the stem, not down towards the bud, which could become diseased. Where buds are in pairs opposite each other, make a horizontal cut above both buds.

🌿 Cut too far from a bud and the stub of stem above the bud may die (known as die-back). The entire shoot could then die off, so if you spot die-back, it's best to cut it out. Cut too close to a bud and the bud will dry out and die.

WHICH BUD IS WHICH?

Fruit buds are usually plump and rounded, leaf buds small and pointed.

SENSE AND SENSORY

Trickling water, fragrant jasmine, cool grass beneath bare feet, the vivid reds of a graceful Japanese maple in autumn. All gardens are sensory, but here are a few ideas to up the sensual quotient in yours.

SOUND AND VISION

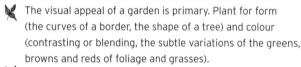 The visual appeal of a garden is primary. Plant for form (the curves of a border, the shape of a tree) and colour (contrasting or blending, the subtle variations of the greens, browns and reds of foliage and grasses).

Use an architectural feature or specimen shrub as a focal point. Draw the gaze around the garden with paths or steps. Create mystery with screens. Add interest with containers and raised beds at different heights and levels (see page 63).

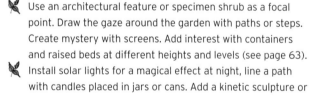 Install solar lights for a magical effect at night, line a path with candles placed in jars or cans. Add a kinetic sculpture or grow swaying bamboo for movement.

Create a soundscape with a wind instrument made from different-sized plastic bottles – cut different-sized slits in the sides and mount on sticks. Hang wind chimes. Leaves and ornamental grasses rustle softly in the breeze. Gravel provides a satisfying crunch beneath the feet, but nothing can beat the soothing sound of water trickling down a mini-cascade or the sound of bees buzzing about their business – plant to attract them (see page 84).

HEAVEN SCENT

Scent is deeply evocative, taking you back instantly to a time and place. Ensure your garden remains memorable by planting mock orange, jasmine, lilac, lily of the valley, sweet violet, hyacinth, pinks, sweet peas, daphne, oriental lilies, roses, lemon verbena or chocolate cosmos.

Fragrant climbers include wisteria, honeysuckle, trachelospermum, clematis; groundcover plants include golden oregano, creeping thyme and sweet woodruff.

Position plants with a strong night-time scent beside a gate or doorway to welcome you home in the evening: night-scented stocks, *Nicotiana sylvestris*, tuberose, four o'clock flower, evening primrose or night phlox.

For a scented window box try petunias, heliotrope, sweet alyssum, and herbs such as mint, sweet basil, lemon thyme or sweet marjoram. Just open the window and breathe in. Release the scent of scented leaf geraniums and any number of herbs by rubbing their leaves between your fingers.

Note: Check before you buy; not all varieties are scented.

For great taste sensations, see pages 62 and 95. And don't forget edible flowers such as nasturtiums, pansies and evening primrose.

FEELING GOOD

All plants are tactile, Stroke the soft, velvety lamb's ear and verbascum, run the aptly named string of pearls plant that feels like beads through your fingers. Plunge your hands into woolly thyme, cup a delicate Chinese lantern in your palm, run your hands over the bark of a tree. Wiggle bare toes in springy grass or moss, feel grasses brushing against bare legs in a wildlife meadow (see page 82).

COTTAGE GARDEN

The quintessential English garden, all potting sheds, vicars and tea on the lawn. In reality cottage gardens are unstructured and informal, often small, with a mix of flowers, shrubs, climbers, fruit and veg ... and more flowers.

I PREDICT A RIOT

Years ago, every bit of the cottage garden had to be productive. That ethos lives on today, though now more for pleasure than subsistence and the ideal garden is a riot of abundance and colour. But organized chaos needs planning.

Group several of the same plant together and plant in drifts. Plant borders to ascend in height, shorter at the front, taller at the back. The kitchen garden is stereotypically confined to the end of a plot, but why not mix edible with ornamental - fruit and veg have flowers, too. Scarlet runner beans make an attractive feature grown up a wigwam of canes. Wild strawberries make good edging plants or groundcover.

Originally, walls, hedges and fences were to keep foxes out and chickens in, but today can also be a decorative element. Low picket fences look particularly charming, as do stone walls with small flowers growing in crevices (ivy-leaved toadflax, self-heal, alpines - nothing too buxom with roots that might force stones apart). Disguise taller walls or those that are not rustic enough with climbers grown up trellises, or train a fruit tree as an espalier. Hedges take a couple of years to grow (plant in early autumn) and need trimming, but provide a home for wildlife. Fast-growing evergreen hedge plants include laurel and photinia.

FAR FROM THE MADDING CROWD

Arches and pergolas covered with climbers (grape vine, solanum, wisteria) add structure and look romantic, leading the way to a secluded natural pond or providing shelter for a garden bench. Decorative features include terracotta pots and other weathered containers (nothing too smart), birdbaths, an old gate or a wheelbarrow.

Paths and stepping stones meander rather than go straight and ideally are wide enough for two people, or just one with a wheelbarrow (or drinks tray). Allow border plants to tumble attractively over the edges (lavender, forget-menots, aubrietia). Plant low-growing creeping varieties among the cracks of paving to soften hard edges (creeping Jenny, Corsican mint, creeping thyme).

EASY-GOING

Use flowering shrubs (lilac, mock orange, forsythia, hydrangea, weigela) and perennials, with annuals (nasturtium, cosmos, cornflower, zinnia) filling in the gaps. If the whole of your plot is covered in plants it won't need too much maintenance. Deadhead to keep flowers coming and keep an eye out for weeds. Support plants that are just a bit too untidy, even for a cottage garden – the art is to install the support before it is needed so the plant grows around it and still looks natural.

Other popular cottage garden plants include, in rough order of ascending height: primroses, violets, marigolds, pinks, periwinkle, geranium, aster, salvia, columbine, hosta, sweet William, euphorbia, veronica, tickseed, scabious, monarda, poppy, peony, lavender, phlox, allium, daisy, lady's mantle, helenium, cone flower, dahlia, delphinium, yarrow, rose, lupin, hollyhock, foxglove, delphinium and sunflower.

A CUT ABOVE

Cut flowers add instant cheer to the home but can be expensive and the choice limited. Grow your own and you won't have to wait for a special occasion to have flowers around the house.

FABULOUS FLOWER FEST

Most cut-flower plants like to be grown in the sun, so in summer you really are spoilt for choice, unlike in winter when the pickings are much more slim. Happily, many bulbs flower in spring and you can get annuals off to an early start by sowing seed under cover (see page 40). Perennials produce flowers year after year, usually with the minimum of fuss, and shrubs, especially evergreens, provide foliage as well as flowers. Don't overlook attractive seed heads as part of an arrangement, adding interest, variety and more bang for your buck (rose hip, oriental poppy), or flowers to dry (statice, helichrysum).

If you have enough room to devote part of your garden to cut flowers, choose a site in the sun, weed it thoroughly and dig in plenty of compost/organic matter before planting. Plant several of the same flower together, so that when you cut some stems, one or two remain in order not to look too 'gappy'.

Some flowers (daffodils, roses, anemones) can be cut in the bud stage (but not too tight), to open in the vase.

YOUR FLOWER YEAR

This random selection is ordered roughly in season – 'roughly' because some are real troupers, straddling more than one. Their flowering also depends upon your local conditions.

Annuals Many make great cut flowers and are scented too. Try sweet peas, cornflowers, snapdragons, stocks, larkspur, aster, bells of Ireland (also can be dried), zinnia, cosmos or nigella.

Bulbs Agapanthus, allium, Peruvian lily (tall variety), camassia, oriental lilies, freesia, iris, gladioli, nerine, Star of Bethlehem, harlequin flower, bugle lily, not forgetting tulips and daffodils.

Spring Hellebore, peony, camellia, Japanese quince (Chaenomeles), forsythia, peony, lily of the valley, anemone and molucella.

Summer Coreopsis, scabious, calendula, blanket flower, Leucanthemum, astrantia, dicentra, gypsophila, perennial sage, linaria, yarrow, rose, garden phlox, monarda, loosestrife, coral bells, goldenrod, gaillardia, globe thistle and euphorbia.

Autumn Rudbeckia, Japanese anemone, purple coneflower, crocosmia, dahlia, honeywort, blue spiraea, chrysanthemum, sedum and penstemon; honesty and Chinese lantern for their seed pods.

Winter Daphne, witch hazel, mahonia, Christmas rose and winter jasmine.

CUT OUT FOR A LONG LIFE

1 Cut flowers in the morning, when it's cooler.

2 Use a clean vase and fresh, cool water. Change the water and re-snip the stems every day.

3 Just before arranging, re-cut stems underwater, at an angle, with a sharp, clean blade. Make an additional vertical cut, 2cm (¾in) up, through the base of woody stems.

4 Remove the bottom leaves so only the stems sit in water.

5 Position out of direct sunlight, ideally somewhere cool.

6 Cut-flower food helps prolong life and zaps any bugs in the water, but there are also many granny-knows-best tactics to try.

Danger, daffs! Their sap is harmful to other flowers. If using in a mixed arrangement, stand daffodils in water containing cut-flower food for several hours first, but don't then recut the stems.

THE ORDER OF THINGS

The opposite of the cottage garden; here everything is neat and symmetrical and nature is controlled. Think elegance and balance, think bewigged courtiers perambulating the parterres of a French château.

BACKYARD VERSAILLES

Formal gardens don't just have flowerbeds, they have parterres. Creating one of these may be out of the question, but a small knot garden should be feasible. Knot gardens are small, distinct sections of garden enclosed in a square frame (usually made of low hedging such as box, *Gaultheria cuneata*, lavender). Inside the frame a symmetrical pattern is marked out in more low hedging, creating smaller compartments within, often planted with low-growing herbs and aromatics (perfect for a small herb garden), or even just laid with coloured gravel.

Parterres, on the other hand, are not really flowerbeds, but knot gardens on a grander scale. They were originally intended to be viewed from above (from the window of your stately home, naturally) to fully appreciate the design. Or create a sunken garden, which adds interest via the change in level. Again it should be ordered and symmetrical, not just a recycled pond, containing neat flowerbeds, paving, a lawn, water feature - a garden within a garden.

KNOT A LOT

If you don't want to go to such lengths, restricting the range of plants grown and following a colour scheme reinforces formal design, as does planting areas to a uniform height. Individual beds can also be planted for seasonal interest - a winter bed, spring, etc. Keep things simple. Separate your plot into defined areas using low walls, fences or hedges, separated by paving. The planting within these areas can still be quite varied and unstructured - or more regimented, if you want to go the whole full-on formal hog.

THE BEST THINGS COME IN PAIRS

Paths are straight and weed-free, perhaps lined with small, clipped shrubs. Keep lawns mown and edges tidy. Ponds are symmetrical with neat edges, ideally a central feature. Use decorative items in pairs - two topiary shrubs placed either side of a doorway or gate, specimen trees in containers either side of a path or at the bottom of steps. Other features to include are sundials, birdbaths, urns, statues (but no gnomes), or even a stone obelisk that will get the neighbours muttering about delusions of grandeur.

GREEN INVESTMENT

Formal gardens are high-maintenance. Hedges need regular clipping, as does topiary, where shrubs are clipped into cones, globes or spirals. Dense, slow-growing foliage is best (box, yew, privet). Use canes and wire as a guide when cutting or to train stems in a particular direction. Work from the top downwards and from the centre outwards.

LOW-MAINTENANCE GARDEN

If you'd much rather spend your free time enjoying your garden than working on it, low maintenance is the way to go. But it needn't mean non-stop paving and patios, unless you're planning on renting out off-street parking.

LOW MAINTENANCE, HIGH IMPACT

Nor need it be bland and boring, but it does involve a little planning and work at the outset. You can choose:

 Walls and fences over hedges that need clipping (hedges need clipping more regularly than fences need painting).

 Slow-growing hedging (box, holly, yew) that requires less attention from the clippers over faster-growing (photinia, cherry laurel, thuya).

 Paving/gravel/decking (or artificial turf) instead of lawn, or part of your lawn. But be aware that this has a negative impact on the environment, contributing to flooding in heavy rain and reducing wildlife habitat.

 A meadow lawn (see page 82) over a mown lawn.

 Grasses, shrubs and perennials (come back each year) over annuals and bedding plants (which must be grown, planted, maintained and removed every year).

 Hardy over tender plants that need tucking up under cover over winter.

 Large containers/hanging baskets that dry out less quickly than small ones.

WORK IT OUT

Use permanent edging for lawns. Check the pH of your soil (see page 17) and plant to your conditions rather than struggle with plants that just don't want to be there (like a pet at the vet's); see what grows well in neighbours' gardens. Cut down on time spent weeding: weed borders in early spring and mulch (see page 65) to suppress new weeds, or plant through a permeable membrane (cut a hole in the membrane) hidden beneath a layer of bark/gravel.

Avoid needy plants that require a lot of attention. Plant borders with shrubs (skimmia, rosemary, camellia, lavatera, ceanothus, cistus, dogwood, viburnum, fuchsia, pieris, hebe) and perennials that can be left to their own devices but won't look untidy (salvia, bleeding heart, rudbeckia, phlox, brunnera, cranesbill, coneflower, hosta, sedum, lantana, penstemon, tickseed and ornamental grasses.)

Position water outlets where they're likely to be most useful. Install a water butt behind a green screen for easy watering in a front garden (see page 106). Invest in an automatic watering system.

Have fewer containers or group them together for one-stop watering.

Use slow-release fertilizer (applied once at the start of the growing season) or liquid plant feed applied during watering (wash 'n' grow).

Go wildlife to be both low-maintenance and eco-friendly (see page 84). Leave seed heads and berries to feed birds in winter. Go no-dig for fruit and veg (see page 62) to save time and your back. Avoid fancy-trained espalier and cordon fruit and opt for natural fruit bushes and trees.

SHADY IN THE CITY

Shade can be a problem in small urban gardens, where closely packed buildings can cast large amounts of shade. Add a couple of trees and the result is like the bottom of the rainforest, but without the juggernaut-sized creepy crawlies.

SHADY DEALINGS

Shade varies from light and dappled to dense, but most shady sites receive at least some light at some time during the day. Damp shade is the easiest to deal with, while dry shade is trickier. The key is to choose the right plants. They may take a while to settle in, but the upside is that unless you opt for a formal garden design, once established, shady gardens are usually fairly low maintenance – sun-loving weeds grow less well in shade, too.

WATERHOLICS

The incredible hulks of the plant world, trees don't need anger management but do have an issue with drink (at least, with water) and also use up lots of nutrients. Improve the soil beneath them by digging in organic matter. If the soil is compacted and difficult to dig due to roots, mulch with a thick layer of organic matter instead. Alternatively, falling leaves from deciduous trees may do the job for you, creating a carpet of nutritious leaf mould. If planting directly in the soil is out of the question, put your shade-tolerant plants in containers instead, or even make a raised bed (see page 63) beneath a tree.

GRASS ROOTS

Grass grows poorly in shade. If the site receives some light, try shade-tolerant lawn seed/turf, and feed spring and autumn. Don't mow too closely and watch out for moss. Or opt for ground cover plants or even artificial turf. Soil shaded by a wall may be dry if shielded from rain. Dig in a generous layer of organic matter to help retain moisture, water regularly and mulch in spring.

SELF-CONTAINED

Plant fruit and veg in containers to stand in your sun hotspots and move them around to follow it, like a reality TV star topping up a perma-tan. Some beans, lettuce, pumpkins, cucumbers and rhubarb will cope with a little shade, especially in summer, so be choosy with varieties.

SHADY CHARACTERS

Shade-tolerant plants include:

Dry Foxglove, Japanese laurel, ivy, mahonia, *Acanthus mollis* (bear's breeches), bugle, bergenia, bleeding heart, lungwort, epimedium (bishop's hat), foam flower, fatsia.

Damp Camellia, daphne, elder, monarda, sweet Cecily, hosta, platycodon, cyclamen, bergenia, hellebore, day lily, globe flower, astilbe, foxglove, anemone, winter aconite, viola.

Try reducing the amount of shade by cutting back or thinning offending trees/shrubs. Boost what light there is by whitewashing walls and using mirrors.

WHERE THE WILD THINGS GROW

Great for biodiversity and wildlife, wildflower meadows are a mix of wildflowers and grasses left to grow naturally. Grow a mini-meadow on a small patch 1m² (10¾ square feet), or in a trough.

ANNUAL OR PERENNIAL?

Unlike annual wildflowers, perennials do better on less fertile soil. Usually smaller and more delicate, on fertile soil they're edged out by beefier species.

Annual meadows usually flower early summer to autumn, when they die back, although the seed they shed will germinate the following spring. Useful for sowing on a neglected area of garden or even for filling gaps in a border as they tolerate the more fertile existing garden soil. Perennial meadows flower from spring through to summer and work well grown as an alternative to grass, to replace a whole or part of a lawn.

STARTING FROM SCRATCH

Both annual and perennial meadow seed mixes are available. Annual meadows are best sown from seed – follow the packet instructions. Dig over a site that's not too damp or shady, remove large stones and thuggish perennial weeds (see page 66) and rake to a fine tilth. If sown in spring, some seeds won't germinate until the following year, so autumn may be better.

MEADOW MAKEOVER

To transform an existing lawn, check out the grass. Broad, tall leaves in clumps are couch/rye grass, which will be too strong for the meadow varieties. Remove the turf entirely, or rotivate and dig it in, then sow. If the leaves are fine, narrow and not in clumps, rake over the lawn vigorously to create gaps of bare soil for the seed, then sow as directed.

If removing the top layer of too-fertile soil sounds too drastic, try adding yellow rattle seed to the seed mix (some mixes already contain it); it weakens tough grasses, allowing flowers to come through.

Wildflower plug plants can be planted at more or less any time (if the ground is not frozen) among freshly sown seed or in an existing lawn, 5–6 per m² (10¾ sq. ft). Keep watered until established.

CONTINUE THE LOOK

Perennials and grasses planted in drifts in borders continue the natural meadow feel. Decorate with the odd cow – or more realistically an old gate, wheelbarrow, weathered bench, swing, a fruit tree for a mini-orchard...

Sow a meadow in a trough using loam-based compost mixed with garden soil. Use a seed mix, or plant native wildflowers or similar species.

Year 1
Mow a few times during the growing season to 5-8cm (2-3in).

Year 2 onwards
Summer-flowering Mow August/September after the plants have shed their seed. Rake up the cuttings or the soil fertility will be improved (OMG!).
Spring-flowering Cut after the seed has been shed, then every 3 weeks or once in late summer. Dig out/spot treat perennial weeds.

For an instant mini-meadow, buy a section of wildflower turf that is pre-grown with wildflowers (lay spring or autumn). Water well and watch it grow.

ATTRACTING WILDLIFE

We're not talking jeeps and khaki-clad guides: even the most modest of gardens can have a corner dedicated to attracting local wildlife – within reason. Ratty types need not apply.

COME ON IN

Everyone knows bees are a very good thing. As well as producing delicious honey and that beautiful buzzy sound, they are vital for pollination. Different bees (there are many species) like different flowers – some like flat flowers (aster, cosmos, zinnia ... great for an easy landing), some like tubular flowers (foxgloves, snapdragons, penstemon, campanula). They also particularly like the colour purple (lavender, catmint, rosemary, salvia). Open a bee B&B with a hive or a bee house, a kind of bee condo for solitary, emo bees (in a warm but shaded spot) that hate communal living.

HERE BIRDY, BIRDY

Hedges and trees provide shelter and roosting and nesting areas for birds. Bird feeders range from elaborate feeding stations to feeders that attach to windows and window boxes. Position away from predators and protect from other wildlife that might like to get in on the act (a baffle stops squirrels shinning up a feeding-station pole). Important: keep feeders, tables and water clean to avoid disease.

Position bird nesting boxes in a sheltered spot, away from predators, out of strong sunlight to avoid overheating, unless shaded by a tree or the eaves of a roof. Tilt them forward slightly so rain cannot enter. Once the birds have stopped using the nest, remove it. Harsh? Yes, especially after all the construction effort, but nests harbour fleas and parasites that will infect the next inhabitants. Then pour boiling water over the inside of the box and leave to dry (don't use insecticides/flea powders).

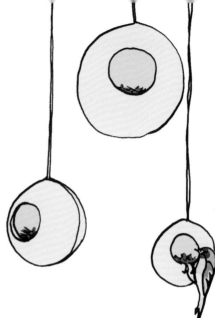

Install a webcam to watch wildlife nocturnal antics or inside a nesting box to springwatch from the comfort of your own laptop.

NOT JUST THE FURRY OR FEATHERED KIND

 Many insects go out to work in the garden every day on our behalf, helping pollination and controlling pest insects. Make it easy for these unsung heroes by not being super-tidy: leave piles of logs and leaves as shelter and restrict or don't use pesticides (go organic). Plant in a sunny, sheltered site to attract beneficial insects: ladybirds like cosmos and yarrow, among others; lacewings fennel and dill. Butterflies love phlox, blanket flower, golden rod, tickseed, rudbeckia, cone flower, monarda, aster, butterfly weed, lantana, passion flower, buddleia... Other plants loved by insects include verbena, marjoram, sedum, thyme and scabious.

Don't forget wildflower meadows (see page 82) and ponds (see page 24). Pondlife you may attract includes dragonflies, damselflies and water boatmen, or newts, frogs and toads that snack on slugs. Ensure one side of the pond slopes to help creatures enter or exit if they fall in. The more adventurous wildlife fan could install a hedgehog home, bat box or owl box.

Don't forget to provide clean water: it is important not just for birds and other creatures to drink and bathe in, but also for insects in their pupal stage.

CHAPTER THREE
THE NO-GARDEN GARDEN

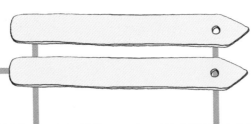

THINKING OUTSIDE THE BOX

Traditional horizontal, ground-floor gardens are not the only gardens in town (or country). Any surface can become a garden – even vertical ones. A balcony, patio, roof terrace, stoop, set of steps or deck can become a flourishing and productive green (and red, yellow, pink, lilac) space; so can a wall or a fence.

TOP OF THE POTS

Plants decorate and add a touch of living colour to the home. Install enough and it will be like being outside without the rain. For an effective display, group several together.

Indoor plants are good for you. They help to purify the air, filtering out some of the common volatile organic compounds (VOCs), such as benzene, formaldehyde and trichloroethylene. These nasty-sounding substances are leached out into the air from upholstery, carpets, paint, plastics, rubber, adhesives ... the list goes on. All indoor plants purify the air to some extent, but the peace lily, dracaena, areca and mother-in-law's tongue are particularly good at it.

HOUSEPLANT HAPPY

When you buy a plant, follow the guide supplied and ask the nursery for advice on how to keep it happy. The chart on pages 90–91 gives you a care package for a rewarding selection of houseplants.

There are two aspects to the type of light that a houseplant needs - the number of hours of light it receives and the intensity. Only cacti and succulents (although pelargoniums are also very tolerant) can put up with continuous bright summer sun. Flowering plants usually like direct sun for a time, while the remainder prefer bright but not direct light, and some will tolerate semi-shade. Most don't like draughts, like your aged relative, and like to be fairly warm (18-21ºC). They can put up with low temperatures for a time but won't thrive.

Watering requirements vary, but a general guide is to insert a finger into the compost and water if it feels dry. Don't overwater; plants can droop due to too much as well as too little water. Don't leave a plant sitting in water. If it is totally parched, soak the pot in a bucket of water for an hour or two, then drain. Tropical plants and orchids, ferns, and bromeliads enjoy a daily mist spray of water.

Rehome in a bigger pot with fresh compost (mix in some slow-release fertilizer granules) when the roots fill the pot. Top-dress in spring - remove the top layer of old, tired compost and replace it with fresh compost, full of nutrients.

Feed with liquid feed during the growing period - flowering plants around once a week, foliage plants around every four weeks, but follow the manufacturer's instructions.

PLANT NAME	☀️☁️	💧	🌡️	🚿
Peace lily (*Spathiphyllum*)	Medium-low indirect light	1	18-25ºC	2
Moth orchid (*Phalaenopsis*)	Indirect, bright light	1	19-30ºC	12
African violet (*Saintpaulia*)	Moderate-bright indirect light	1	18-26ºC with humidity	Weekly
Spider plant (*Chlorophytum comosum*)	Indirect, bright light	1	13-18ºC	Min. 12
Kentia palm (*Howea forsteriana*)	Indirect, medium-bright light	1	16-24ºC	6
Gerbera (*Gerbera jamesonii*)	Bright light in mornings only	1 in warmer months	10-20ºC	Every month during spring and summer
Citrus (such as kumquat, lime, lemon)	Bright sun	1+ in warmer months	10-24ºC	Regular from spring to late autumn
Watermelon begonia (*Peperomia argyreia*)	Medium-low light (and fluorescent lighting)	1 (but don't overwater)	18-24ºC	Monthly in spring and summer
Mother-in-law's tongue *Sansevieria*	Bright light with some sun, but tolerates shade	1 (but don't overwater); much less in winter	16-24ºC	2-3 times during growing season

✔ ✔ ✔	Hard to kill	Easy	Water when leaves start to wilt if you forget to do it before!
✔	Medium	Medium	Do not let the pot sit in water or roots will rot.
✔ ✔ ✔	Medium	Easy	Keep soil moist but not soggy, water with room temperature water from the bottom.
✔ ✔ ✔	Very hard to kill	Easy	Keep soil moist but do not overwater.
✔ ✔ ✔	Medium	Hard (from seed)	They like humidity and water-misting but don't overwater - check soil for moisture regularly.
✔ ✔ ✔	Medium-easy	Don't bother	Too much harsh direct sunlight damages the plant.
✔ ✔	Medium-easy	Easy	Mist the leaves in the morning and put on a tray of wet pebbles. Frost-tender, but can go on the balcony in warm weather.
✔	Hard	Easy	Overwatering can cause root rot, and temperatures that are too low can cause leaf drop.
✔ ✔ ✔	Hard	Easy	Overwatering in winter will cause rot at the base and yellow leaves.

KEY TO SYMBOLS

Sun/shade

Watering (per week)

Temperature

Feeding (per year)

Green effect

Kill factor

Propagating

Staying alive

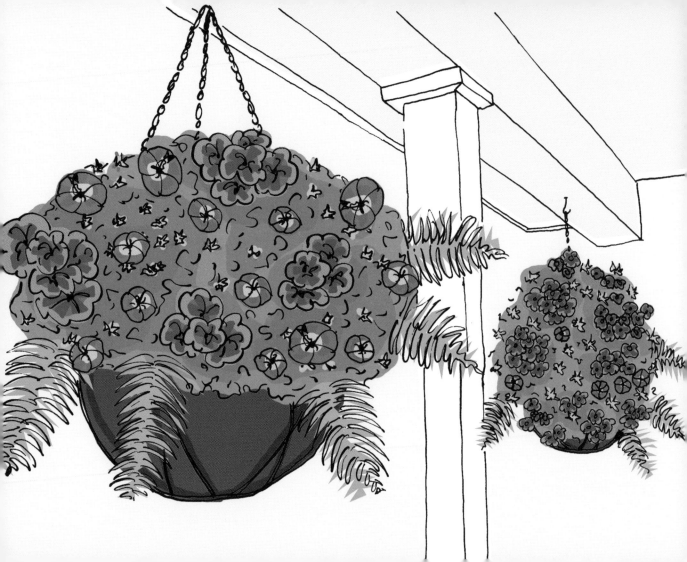

BASKET CASES

Hanging baskets make lovely, eye-level mini-gardens, both indoors and out, and work well on a balcony cascading with strawberries, tomatoes or dwarf veg or sprouting with spring flowers and succulents.

Most containers can be suspended, but traditional hanging baskets are made from open-sided wire-mesh, rattan or plastic; they also come in terracotta (cone shapes are particularly lovely), cast-iron and ceramic. They can be simple or sophisticated, cheap or more expensive, with inbuilt watering systems. They do require some preparation and maintenance but are well worth the investment.

BASKET CANDIDATES

Try begonias, busy lizzies, impatiens, nicotiana, laurentia, viola (pansies), geraniums and bidens, with trailing plants such as nasturtiums, lobelia, ivy-leaved geraniums, petunias and trailing fuschia or ferns at the edge. Go high in the centre, mound-round around and full-on cascade at the edges. Go for colour and exuberance. In a 30cm (12in) basket you can plant around 8-10 plants as a rule of green thumb.

PLANTING IN THE AIR

Once the frosts have gone, be a positive basket case. Here's a handy how-to guide to getting the hang of an open-sided basket.

1 Sketch out your colour and planting scheme and take advice on plants.

2 Keep your basket steady in a bucket while you fill it.

3 Line with your liner of choice (for example, wood fibre liner, moss), press in place, and puncture at the sides for trailing plants, making slits around 5cm (2in) in length.

4 Add a layer of multi-purpose compost mixed with water gel crystals and slow-release (organic) fertilizer granules, level with the lowest slits.

5 Plant your trailing plants head first, root last through the holes from the inside and gently tweak the roots.

6 Add more compost and continue planting, placing an upright, bushy plant in the middle or a really striking centrepiece.

7 Leave a green finger's width at the top to prevent spillages when watering.

8 Water well after planting.

9 Water daily (twice when it's really hot). A plastic bottle works well as a watering funnel in the centre.

10 Feed, water and deadhead regularly, and no need to share with the slugs!

NO OUCH POUCH

Ready-to-buy, easy-to-plant hessian, plastic and reusable polypropylene planting pouches can be hooked easily onto railings, fences and walls for colourful displays.

Reusable, liner-free baskets with removable panels and built-in reservoirs for watering are a fuss-free, pre-prepped alternative. A lantern with succulents makes a great mini-terrarium for in or outdoors. A selection of perennial herbs (thyme, mint, rosemary) in a colander customized with liner, compost and chains makes a nice hanging herb garden. For those with memories like sieves, plant sensors are available that remind you via an app on Wi-Fi to water your plants.

HANGING IN OVER WINTER

Baskets need care in the chilly months but can still hang in there, so don't give up on winter floral displays. Empty your summer basket once all the flowers have done their stuff, then replant in the early autumn with winter-flowering pansies, cyclamen, violas, primroses, crocus or ivy. Add structure with box or rosemary; try a winter-flowering heather mixed with small-flowered cyclamen and bright pansies. Plant bulbs such as narcissi, snowdrops and alpines. Winter baskets need less watering than their summer equivalents but do keep an eye on the soil as it may dry out in the wind. If so,

plunge it in a bucket of water for a few minutes for a good old soak and then drain.

TAKING ROOT IN THE AIR

Vegetables in hanging baskets save space and supply colour and flavour. Dwarf tomatoes, dwarf beans, snow peas, herbs, mini-cucumbers, peppers, chillies, radishes, small beetroots, dwarf-stumped carrots, spinach, rocket, cut-and-come-again lettuce, even small aubergine varieties can all be grown. Add a trailing plant such as nasturtium or an alpine strawberry for an edible and attractive cascade. Go for a three-tiered set of baskets to expand your salad days. Beware strong winds and frosts and move around to maximize sunlight. Always feed and water well and, if necessary, protect from hungry birds with some netting. Enjoy.

CONTAIN, MAINTAIN, NEVER PLAIN

Pots and containers bring flexibility, fun, formality and food to the smallest outdoor space. They make great focal points too, and with a quick change of colour scheme and arrangement, you can introduce a whole new look each spring. Move around according to needs and conditions (sun, wind, rain). Way to grow.

If you want a touch of frivolity or a flash of fiery colour in a dark corner, choose, paint or decorate your pots in bright hues, but beware mixing too many container styles and colours. You could contain yourself and make a simple yet stunning statement with a single, elegant pot housing a well-maintained plant, tall tulips, a large lily, a Japanese maple, olive, bay or lemon tree.

Almost anything can be transformed into a pot for plants with some imagination and a few holes, from antique, frost-resistant terracotta pots to well-worn Wellington boots and zingy zinc cubes. Terracotta pots are porous and tend to lose more moisture, but their colour complements most plants and weathers nicely. Plastic pots come in almost every hue you can imagine and are lightweight and strong, but thinner than clay, and so offer less insulation and plants can perish sooner. Rust-free, galvanized pots work well, as do other metal containers, such as old tin baths (lined with compost bags), watering cans, milk churns and old galvanized barrels (metal heats in direct sunlight and can warm up the soil and the root ball). Smaller containers come in the form of olive oil and paint tins, food (tomato/coffee/biscuit) cans and old metal buckets (suspended with chains or ropes for extra space). Railing planters with brackets save room and make lovely displays when planted up on the balcony.

GO REALLY POTTY

 Fun, inexpensive containers can be made from plastic or cardboard juice cartons and cola bottles.

 Repurpose hollow breeze blocks, plastic shopping baskets with liners, washing-machine drums, small tyres, birdcages, cake stands, jelly moulds, vintage typewriters, old shoes, bicycle baskets, teapots with no lids, enamel bowls and mugs, metal bread bins, the empty base of an old chair, vintage butler's sinks, an old chandelier, a metal trunk, muffin tins (for moss and small plants) or saucepans - all with drainage holes.

 Turn a second-hand bottle rack (wooden or metal) on its side and make a library of herbs from a cellar of wine.

POT MAINTENANCE

Plants in pots need some TLC. Use a quality, multi-purpose (preferably peat-free) compost for your containers and soil-based compost for trees and long-term plants. Add grit for drainage along with holes in the bottom of the container, and place a few stones, pieces of broken pot or lightweight polystyrene at the bottom of the container. Water and feed regularly with a liquid, high-nitrogen feed (seaweed is good) in the summer months and rotate for even growth. Replace any plants that fail and deadhead regularly. Some bought containers come complete with in-built watering systems. Depending on levels of shade, raise your pots up in height to access more sunlight (easier on the knees too!) and raise the pots off the ground with feet in wet weather. In the winter months, protect your plants with bubble wrap around the pot to protect the roots or fleece around the plant or take them indoors (particularly for citrus fruit etc.). Always remove saucers in winter.

POT DESIGN

Try mixing things up in one of your containers in a three-tiered planting design. Plant a small tree or tallish plant (clematis, fuchsia) in the centre and smaller ones (e.g. pansies, begonias) around it, with a trailing plant (e.g. petunias) or vine around the edge. Rehearse different schemes at the nursery before investing. You might think you want to go rainbow, but then rein it in a bit. Plants of similar hues work well: lavender, geranium, violas and petunias in shades of purple, for example. In a mixed-herb container, a bay tree at the centre with fragrant culinary herbs around it (rosemary, oregano and thyme) makes an impact on the eye, nose and palate. Ornamental grasses can be very effective and bring movement to the balcony.

POT SIZE

Don't put too many plants in one container, and ensure each one has enough room and compost to grow. And think about size: a small plant in a huge pot will look silly and may fail to thrive. On the other hand, bay and olive trees like to have their roots confined, so choose a smaller pot for these than you might think necessary. Ask for advice at the nursery.

EDIBLE BALCONIES

Don't let high living put you off getting down and dirty – growing fruit and veg on your balcony can be the height of delight. First, ask yourself the same questions you would for a ground-floor garden. Is the area windy or sheltered? What impact will my edible balcony have on the neighbours (above/below/to the side)? How much sun will my patch enjoy? If it is at least 4-5 hours per day in the growing season, then it's time to take pot luck.

BALCONY HERB POT

You will need:

- Container compost (organic and peat free with water-retaining granules, if possible)
- Liquid plant food
- Herb seedlings or small plants
- Large pot (at least 35cm/13¾in deep) or wooden veg box. Make sure it has holes in the bottom, or drill some if you need to
- Layer of stones or broken pots (for drainage)
- Watering can

Place the broken pots or stones at the bottom of your container. Add some compost mixed with water-retaining granules, if using, position the seedlings or plants – don't crowd them, they need space to grow. Fill in around the plants with compost to around 2.5cm (1in) below the rim, then firm. Water well but gently (see page 41). Containers dry out quickly, particularly in warm weather, so water regularly to keep the soil moist (but not saturated). Once the plants are established, feed with liquid fertilizer during the growing period. Look out for pests, including aphids and whitefly.

GROW YOUR OWN HIGH-ALTITUDE SALAD

Lettuce and mixed leaves, rocket, spinach, radishes, tomatoes, spring onions, parsley, chives, chillies, coriander, bok choy, pea shoots.

INFUSIASTIC

Grow your own tea chest (or cocktail cabinet) using mint, lemon verbena, lemon basil and other culinary herbs. All you need is to add for a mojito is the rum...

MICRO-FARMING ON A BALCONY

Grow carrots, potatoes and other root vegetables in grow bags or sacks on the smallest of balconies. Plant potatoes in terracotta pots, dustbins or even a black plastic bag and avoid attack by pests. Plant early varieties to avoid blight. If all you have is a windowsill, a sprouting seed kit is no mean have-bean solution, and can keep you supplied with power-packed foods, such as mung beans, fenugreek, alfalfa, buckwheat and watercress.

WEIGHT TO GO

Watch out for safety issues when composing your edible balcony or rooftop. Make sure all your pots are securely fastened and any hanging baskets firmly chained in place. And when watering, check you are not raining on anyone else's parade. Always ensure your pots have adequate drainage and put saucers, old plates or lids under your pots to prevent water running onto and then off the balcony.

ALL THE Ws

Welfare Don't let your plants dry out or they will wilt and wane. Feed and water regularly and ensure the pots are deep enough for the plants so that the roots are not crushed (around 15cm (6in) for salads and 35cm (13¾in) for root veg).
Wind and wheels Check out the wind factor and protect your plants. Move the pots around if necessary to maximize sun and minimize wind exposure. Use a wheelbarrow to transport your pots if space allows.

Weight-watchers Don't overload your balcony with too many heavy pots. To make larger pots lighter, put upturned plastic plant pots in the base before filling or use a soil-less potting compost.

Which Think what you are most likely to use before you include in your perched potager garden. It may sound obvious but there's no point filling a container with a big selection of herbs if you aren't going to use them.

EASY PEASY

Start with tomato seedlings and progress to growing from seed as confidence takes root (see page 40). Start them off on the windowsill and then move onto the balcony in the warmer weather. Choose a variety that promises a large crop, and with a little luck and about six hours' sunlight a day, the tomatoes will grow quickly in pots and need to be controlled (or pests and diseases will harvest the rewards). Support the plants with stakes and ties (repurpose old tights) or make a cage. Trailing, tumbler tomatoes in a hanging basket are both decorative and delicious. You will need a basket, liner, container compost, water-retaining product, slow-release fertilizer and your tomato plug/seeds plus (importantly) a sunny, sheltered position. Water well. Tomatoes deter mosquitoes so that is a win-win on balconies.

BALCONY CANDIDATES

Cucumber, beans and tomatoes.

Fruit trees (peach, pear, apple) grow well on balconies but need plenty of sun, and it is important to remember weight issues.

Blackberries, blueberries, redcurrants and strawberries can all be grown in containers.

Oranges and lemons and other frost-tender plants need to be moved inside in the chilly months.

THE HEIGHT OF TREND - VERTICAL GARDENING FOR BALCONIES AND ROOF TERRACES

If your horizontal space is limited, think vertically. You too can have a blooming balcony, an edible urban utopia. Brick walls, shed walls, fences: all are potential home for annuals, edibles and even perennials.

Attach pots or tin cans safely to a slatted fence with hooks or wire and you can make a multi-coloured wall of herbs or flowering plants. Use a weatherproof paint in a dark colour to form a stylish backdrop for planting. Buy or repurpose your own shoe organizer. Also available (or DIY-able) is a tiered planter structure on casters with drainage system, which makes a mobile kitchen garden when planted with salads and herbs. Modular breathable vertical planters are widely available.

DIY DIV

If you don't have a spare bare wall, improvise. Attach wire netting to a wooden frame and hang smallish pots. Rows of terracotta pots full of herbs look stunning. Buy or make a living picture, a frame divided into planting cells with small succulent cuttings or even moss.

Repurpose plastic storage boxes from a well-known Scandinavian furniture supplier, whose plastic bag holders also make great vertical planters. Once you get the hang of vertical gardening you could investigate a vertical aquaponic system for growing vegetables without soil in columns above a fish tank, but that is for more advanced verti-growers. Freestanding flower towers with internal watering systems are also available.

Pallets or wooden or plastic crates stacked on top of each other make a great set of green shelves. For extra Zen, you could have a small pond below. An old chest of drawers with the drawers pulled out at different levels is an upcycled garden with knobs on.

Paint it a bright colour with contrasting plants or different colours with plants to match.

Put pots on the steps of a nicely repurposed and painted ladder for an easy upright option. Upcycled rain gutters (complete with drainage holes) can be attached to a fence and filled with trailing plants.

Green walls can be purchased, with plants pregrown in panels, but they require investments of time and money.

If you have some of the latter and none of the former, you could buy rolls of artificial foliage to attach to a large unsightly wall or one that gets no sun.

GREEN SCREEN

A green screen, living wall, structural fence or 'fedge' (fence with climbing plants) – all these make vertical divisions or boundaries that perform a variety of functions. They can hide unsightly views or structures, protect the garden from noise, high winds and nosiness, and soften hard edges (such as metal or concrete). They bring privacy, intimacy and can be focal points in themselves.

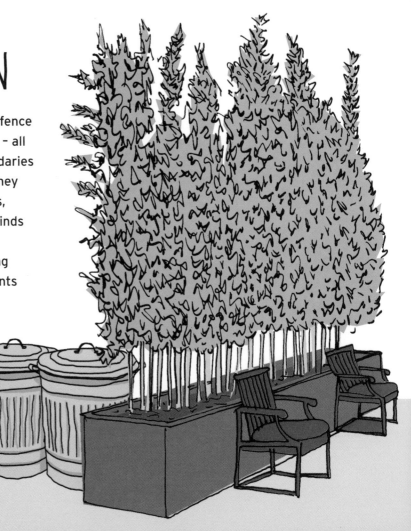

To create screens on a patio or within a garden, plant your green screen in planters - either in individual containers or one long planter, metal bin or trough. Don't be afraid to make a design feature of the container itself. Be bold with colours and shapes.

Hedging plants and shrubs (hydrangea, spruce, viburnum) make a good screen. Fences, trellis or pergolas (inherited or installed) are good for fast-growing annual or perennial vines.

Evergreens will give you privacy all year round, but deciduous plants will lose their foliage in late autumn and winter. You could layer your planting to cover all angles.

Measure your space to get to know your boundaries and make sure you are aware how big your selected greenery will grow. Check it won't invade your neighbour's space (talk over the fence, literally) and establish which way your wall faces using a compass. You can then determine how much sun and shade your plant will be exposed to and choose accordingly. It is useful to get advice from the nursery at this point so you don't waste money and time. For advice on planting by a wall, see page 59.

iDANGER

Russian vine, Chinese wisteria and grape vine can take over, so beware.

iBAMBOOBOO

A ready-made bamboo screen can be very effective but be careful of planting bamboo as it can be very invasive.

iCLIMB

Good trellis climbers include honeysuckle, wisteria, roses, sweet peas and clematis. And you will get added fragrance too. Result.

iFRUIT

If your screen gets lots of sun, you could consider a fruit tree (such as apple, pear, fig) or a pre-trained espalier.

iCREEP

Virginia creeper doesn't need any support at all but can be quite invasive, so beware. Shade-loving ivy and self-clinging hydrangea will also do some good free climbing but are good at finding their way into cracks, so check your walls and brickwork.

ONE
STOOP
BEYOND

If your 'garden' is a set of steps or metal stairs, don't despair. Stoop gardening has advantages. Although relatively low-maintenance, a flight of flowers can be high-impact. It is the equivalent of your front garden, so make a step-by-step first and lasting impression and feed and water regularly to keep it looking good, but don't block the exit if it is a fire escape.

TAKE IT UP A LEVEL

Upcycle containers: use upturned ceramic pots, drainage tiles or terracotta chimneys as stands for extra height but ensure they are securely in position. Add a mosaic effect to a terracotta pot with pieces of broken pottery or glass for added colour, texture and reflected light. Use mirrors on basement walls with steps to increase the sense of space. Tile your steps for extra effect and match with the containers.

Intersperse plants with solar-powered lamps or candles in lanterns (safely) in the evening. There's always the risk that someone will be so green with envy that they will pinch not only your ideas but your pots too. Make them as heavy as possible to deter thieves, and attach them to each other with wire or to railings if applicable.

Position a planter on either side of your flight of steps, up or down, to define your entrance, allowing for guests and mail deliveries. Go minimalist with a limited palette of plant and pots, maybe on just one side, or choose an array of colours, sizes and shapes. Play with the visual aspects of the plants, their height, shape and trailing potential – much-loved geraniums (pelargoniums) have a scalloped leaf and striking flower, palms will bring vertical interest. Mix and match – the skylight is your limit.

Or go with a single theme. On 'edible steps' grow herbs, tumbling strawberries, vegetables and tomatoes in pots if sunlight permits. Restrict yourself to herbs only and add some chilli plants for 'spicy stoop'. Go 'kitchen-quirky' with repurposed coffee tins, fruit crates, watering cans, vintage milk churns and pre-loved colanders as containers. Sun-loving, low-maintenance cacti would make up an attractive 'succulent stairway', but do protect them from too much rain, heat and cold temperatures by taking them indoors in the wetter, colder months.

A single, elegant feature on either side of your top step brings simple style to an entrance. Think box ball or cone, bay tree, English ivy, ornamental grass, hostas (watch out for slugs) or fern. Or lavender for a fragrant welcome. Topiary brings formality and matching container and door in colour adds extra symmetry and style.

RESOURCES

USEFUL WEBSITES

Royal Horticultural Society
www.rhs.org.uk

Society of Garden Designers
www.sgd.org.uk

National Trust Gardens
www.nationaltrust.org.uk/visit/places/
gardens-and-parks

National Garden Scheme
www.ngs.org.uk

The Good Gardeners Association
goodgardeners.org.uk

Garden Organic gardenorganic.org.uk

BBC gardening website
bbc.co.uk/gardening

Gardening Know How urban gardens
www.gardeningknowhow.com/special/
urban

GARDEN CENTRES

www.wyevalegardencentres.co.uk

www.hillier.co.uk

Check your local area for independent
garden centres

FURTHER READING

The Good Gardener, Simon Akeroyd
(Pavilion Books)

*Gardener's World: 101 Ideas for Small
Gardens*, Martyn Cox (BBC Books)

RHS Gardening Through the Year
(Dorling Kindersley)

The Complete Garden Expert,
D.G. Hessayon (Expert)

RHS The Urban Gardener, Matt James
(Mitchell Beazley)

My Tiny Veg Plot, Lia Leendertz (Pavilion
Books)

*My Tiny Garden: Stylish Ideas for Small
Spaces*, Lucy Scott and Jon Cardwell
(Pavilion Books)

First published in the United Kingdom in 2016 by
Portico
1 Gower Street
London
WC1E 6HD

An imprint of Pavilion Books Company Ltd

ISBN 978-1-91023-282-8

A CIP catalogue record for this book is available from the British Library.

10 9 8 7 6 5 4 3 2 1

Reproduction by Mission Productions Ltd, Hong Kong
Printed and bound by Times Offset (M) Sdn Bhd, Malaysia

This book can be ordered direct from the publisher at www.pavilionbooks.com